Leading and Learning in Schools

Brain-Based Practices

Henry G. Cram and Vito Germinario

The Scarecrow Press, Inc.

Technomic Books

Lanham, Maryland, and London

2000

SCARECROW PRESS, INC.
Technomic Books

Published in the United States of America
by Scarecrow Press, Inc.
4720 Boston Way, Lanham, Maryland 20706
http://www.scarecrowpress.com

4 Pleydell Gardens, Folkestone
Kent CT20 2DN, England

British Library Cataloguing in Publication Information Available

Library of Congress Cataloging-in-Publication Data

Cram, Henry G.
   Leading and learning in schools : brain-based practices / Henry G. Cram and Vito Germinario.
      p. cm.
   Includes bibliographical references and index.
   ISBN 0-8108-3755-2 (paper : alk. paper)
   1. Learning, Psychology of.   2. Brain.   I. Germinario, Vito.   II. Title

   LB1060.C73 2000
   370.15′23—dc21   99–057352

In memory of my mother, Anna Backenroth Cram, and my brothers-in-law David Wiltse and Paul Stetka

Henry Cram

To my family and friends for their love, support, encouragement, and guidance: Thank you for being a part of my life.

Vito Germinario

Contents

Acknowledgments

The authors wish to thank the following: The Rancocas Valley Regional High School and Moorestown Public School systems, whose programs, practices, and dedicated staff provided the framework for this publication, and the many colleagues with whom we have worked and who have motivated us and helped shape our thinking on many of the issues discussed in this volume.

The authors are also indebted to Dr. Patrick Rossi, MD, for his guidance in researching the neurological material contained in this volume; to Adam Dempsey for his assistance in creating many of the illustrations; to Cheryl Haines for her assistance in research and editing; to Dr. Richard Bucko for sharing his knowledge and resources; and to Karen Phillips for typing the manuscript.

CHAPTER 1

Our Growing Understanding
of How We Learn

We are now confronting an explosion of new information about the workings of our brain that will profoundly affect educational policy and practice. Yet our profession, oriented as it is toward the social sciences with only a limited understanding of biology and cognitive science, stands unready at the moment to take advantage of this new revolution.

Robert Sylwester

Teachers have been working with brains from the beginning of time, with only a limited knowledge of how the mind works. Educators have never had the scientists' tools, the time, or the freedom to develop truly scientific methodologies or to conduct the research that would satisfy their curiosity. The solution has been to focus on those behaviors that could be observed and on those outcomes that could be measured. Teachers have had to settle for modifying the manifestations of cognition rather than on developing and strengthening the underlying mechanisms and processes by which a student actually learns. Unable to focus on the internal processes of the brain, educators have manipulated the external objects and events of the environment and gauged their success on the resulting behavior that emerged. As Sylwester (1995) writes, "the practical base of our profession was probably closer to folklore knowledge than scientific knowledge" (p. 3).

For most of our history, the human brain was impenetrable, and even in those instances when the brain itself could be examined, direct observation yielded very little about the mystery of its inner workings. Our

1

exploration of the mind was limited to animal research, studies of individuals with damaged brains or mental illness, or laboratory experiments using normal primates or human subjects. But today, because of sophisticated medical technologies, we are in the midst of a revolution of knowledge about the human brain. Researchers can now explain the functioning of the brain by observing its blood flow, recording its electromagnetic fields, and analyzing its chemical composition. Instrumental techniques such as magnetic resonance imaging (MRI) and computerized axial tomography (CAT) are helping us learn about the chemical composition of the brain's cells and neurotransmitters. Positron emission tomography (PET) traces the distribution of blood as it replenishes energy used in the brain's electrical activity. The electroencephalogram (EEG) and related procedures record the electrical transmission of information along the neural fibers and across synapses that produce maps of the human brain in action, maps that reveal how the parts of the brain are involved in performing a whole range of behaviors, including how it learns.

As a result of the research taking place in cognitive science, neuroscience, the human genome project, physics, and pharmacology, we are in the midst of a knowledge explosion important to teaching and learning, for each field is contributing to the illumination of how the brain collects, processes, interprets, and stores information. Never before have we known more about human learning and never before have we had the potential for increasing our success with a wider range of students. This increased understanding of the human brain should help us improve the way we operate schools. Knowing how students learn will inevitably lead us to more effective ways of teaching.

Educators must prepare to respond to this explosion of new understanding in ways that will avoid the mistakes of the past and identify those educationally significant breakthroughs that will frame emerging theories of learning. Unfortunately this potentially valuable information is not getting into the hands of educational practitioners fast enough. The profession, oriented as it is towards the social and behavioral sciences, stands unready, with its limited knowledge of these new fields of science, to take advantage of this revolution in learning. This research deals with neurons, synapses, chemicals, blood, and tissue, subjects that are unfamiliar to most educators. Their professional training has relied on the social sciences, which teach us little about an individual brain and more about how a group of brains might interact. In short, we need to move beyond what appears now to have been a simplistic and narrow approach to teaching and learning.

Educators must begin to embrace what is being learned about the brain and determine how it can best be applied to what they are teaching, how they are teaching, and how they are assessing what is being learned. But brain research must be carefully examined before the appropriate implications for education can emerge. Not everything that the neuroscientist has discovered comes as a surprise to most teachers; but by adding the biological dimensions we begin to understand why certain things are true. Teachers, for example, have always encouraged students to find patterns and to make connections, and they have always "known" that students learn more when they are emotionally involved. It is not, as Renate Nuemmella Caine and Geoffrey Caine (1991) write, "that we are doing the right or wrong thing; it is more a matter of seeing beyond our ways of doing business" (p. vii). We need a framework to better understand how to make sense of what we have always known and what we are constantly learning.

On the surface, incorporating the findings of cognitive science and neuroscience into a framework of how schools function should not be hard. But getting that framework into the schools and affecting the way schools operate are challenging feats. We must first appreciate the power of the mental models upon which schools operate and how they conflict with the emerging frameworks for brain-compatible teaching and learning.

OUR MENTAL MODELS OF HOW WE LEARN

The emerging body of research into the nature of learning is challenging some of the underlying principles of current learning theory. What we are learning about the human brain and the process of cognition will evolve into a new perspective of what it means to teach and to learn. What we are discovering through brain imaging and the other technologies is helping us understand the human brain at the cellular and systems levels. This expanded knowledge of the brain's functioning will require educators to shift their orientation from the social and behavioral sciences to the emerging cognitive sciences and neurosciences that are beginning to come up with answers to the questions about teaching and learning that have eluded the profession.

Education was designed and continues to operate on what Caine and Caine (1991) call "a cluster of interactive but restrictive assumptions that in operation actually interfere with the teaching/learning process" (p. 12). These assumptions, or mental models, are deeply held beliefs that influence the way we think and determine the actions we take. They are usually so deeply held that we are unaware of their impact upon us and how they limit the way we perceive new information.

Primitive models of the brain have existed for more than two thousand years, dating back to the Greco-Roman metaphor of a hydraulic system and moving on to the enchanted loom of the early Industrial Revolution and the computer analogy of the 1950s of the brain as a serial processor. Most educators, however, are caught in a mental model of teaching and learning derived from the more recent industrial era, the so-called *factory model*. In that model schools are seen as factories and are organized around the tenets of assembly line production. Subjects are separated. Information is delivered. Student assessment is based on the final product of what the student has memorized. From this perspective, information is delivered to the empty minds of passive learners through interventions and techniques designed to impart knowledge, to acquire a skill, or to change a behavior. It is behaviorist in its foundation, in that it reduces what is to be learned to specific and readily identifiable parts and utilizes rewards and punishment to produce the desired outcome. The mental models that permeate most of education presume that experts create knowledge, teachers disseminate knowledge, and students are graded on how much of this knowledge they can retain (Caine and Caine, 1998, p. 10).

Even more modern metaphors for the learning process, such as the brain as a computer, suggest that the learning process is a matter of programming the brain's independent parts for the accumulation of knowledge and the acquisition of skills. But unlike human learners, computers are developed, programmed, and operated by external forces. The way they operate, file, and store information is not comparable to the way the brain processes information.

What we are learning through research on the brain refutes several of the basic assumptions that have framed our mental models of the teaching/learning process:

- Learning is not externally directed but something that learners must do for themselves.
- Learners are not passive recipients of information but choose what they will attend to and remember.
- Emotions are not irrelevant to learning but play a critical part in both attention and memory.
- Content cannot be learned devoid of context and must have personal meaning and relevance to the learner.

Brains are holistic, self-adjusting, interactive neural networks and as Marshall (1998) describes it, "[L]earning is a natural, active, messy process of pattern formulation and constructed meaning" (p. 49).

New, biologically based theories of teaching and learning focus on the developmental relationships between nature and nurture. The debate on the relative importance of each and the presumed dichotomy between the two has been replaced by a belief in the probable interrelationship between the brains of our ancestors and our current environment. What we eventually learn and come to know is most likely the result of a complex interrelationship among evolutionary selection procedures that influenced our brain's architecture, the molecular structure of our DNA (a form of memory that passes from one generation to the next), and the adaptation of our brain to the environment in which we live.

This growing understanding of the theory and research into the mysteries of the human brain will eventually lead us toward creating a more brain-compatible environment in which students will learn more easily and understand more deeply the skills, knowledge, and behaviors needed for successful participation in society. Educational professionals need not be experts on the brain but must have an appreciation of how the brain works so they can more fully understand the complexities of the teaching/learning process.

THE PHYSIOLOGY OF THE BRAIN

Until recently the study of the brain was largely the preserve of philosophers, psychologists and behavioral scientists. Today, however, we are being provided with insights into the physical functioning of the human mind that are challenging our metaphors for, and our mental models about, how we learn. Learning can no longer be imagined as a simple process of self-organization of what we experience. We now know that it is a collaborative process, social in nature, focused on problem-solving activity, and dependent upon the learner's interaction with other learners through involvement and experimentation (Abbott, 1998, p. 18).

The brain is a living and ever-changing organ that grows and reshapes itself in response to the environment and the experiences it encounters. It is the result of thousands of years of human evolution. The adult human brain weighs about three pounds, a large brain relative to our body weight. Although only about 2 percent of our body weight, it consumes 20 percent of the body's energy and oxygen. It is 78 percent water, 10 percent fat, and 8 percent protein. Our blood supplies the brain with nutrients such as glucose, protein, trace elements, and oxygen at a rate of about eight gallons per hour (Jensen, 1998, pp. 8–10). The brain comprises a network of more than 62,000 miles of axons and dendrites that carry chemical messages between the billions of cells and allow it to interpret stimuli, deduce meaning, and initiate responses. Our brain discriminates:

- What is important for us to pay attention to
- What we need to register and store for future use
- How we retrieve that information and adjust to new experiences

This process is the essence of learning.

The human brain contains 100 billion neurons. These cells are connected by sensory motor connections to our body. They synthesize chemicals called *neurotransmitters* that communicate with other neurons to determine our response to internal and external stimuli. Neurons consist of a compact cell body, dendrites, and an axon. The information that each neuron processes is coded into a chemical molecule in the cell body. These chemical messengers, or *neurotransmitters,* carry the message across the *synapse,* which is a narrow gap between the neurons' connecting fibers. Each neuron has *dendrites,* connecting nerve fibers to other cells, that receive information, and a single fiber called an *axon,* which sends the neuron's messages to other cells, propagating action potentials (Sylwester, 1995, pp. 25–33) (figure 1.1).

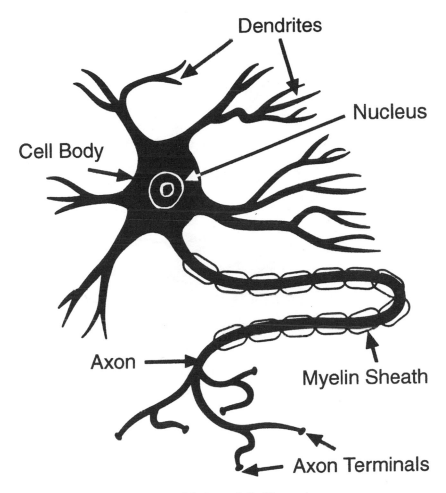

Figure 1.1 *Brain Cells (Neurons)*

The brain also has *glial cells,* or support cells (ten times the number of neurons), which play an important role in establishing the architecture of the brain. These cells form a blood/brain barrier that surrounds the capillaries and denies entrance into the brain of unnecessary or dangerous molecules in the bloodstream. Glial cells are believed to control the brain's immune system and metabolize key

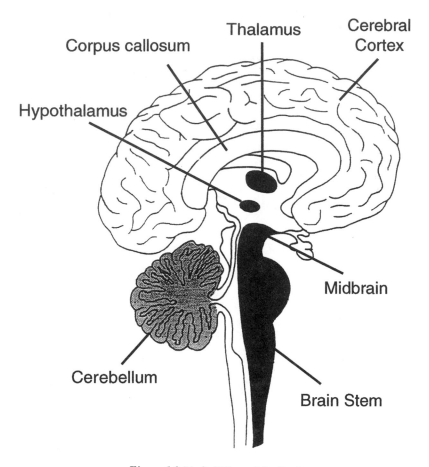

Figure 1.2 Medial View of the Brain

neurotransmitters in the cerebral cortex. They also form the insulating layer (*myelin*) that surrounds the nerve fibers that connect the neurons, a coating that may be connected to the efficiency of neural transmissions.

The most primitive part of the brain is believed to be the *brain stem,* which surrounds the tip of the spinal cord. This root brain regulates basic life functions and contains a set of preprogrammed regulators that keep the body running in ways that ensure its survival (Goleman, 1995, pp. 9–12). It is responsible for our general alertness and serves as an early warning system to the rest of the brain regarding incoming sensory information. This organization leads many neurologists to assert that all learning begins at the sensory level of the cognitive process (Weber, 1998, p. 63).

At the top of the brain stem is the *limbic system,* which provides those chemicals that influence our ability to focus, pay attention, and concentrate. The limbic system is comprised of the *amygdala,* the *hippocampus,* the *thalamus,* and the *hypothalamus.* This area of the brain is believed to be the center for sleep, smell, and our ability to express and mediate our emotions, and is where we combine both internal and external stimuli. The hippocampus serves as a way station for the temporary storage of information; the thalamus appears to be a gateway for the flow of information into the brain (Caine and Caine, 1991, p. 51). The *cerebellum* ("little brain" in Latin) is responsible for balance, position, motor movement, and some areas of cognition (figure 1.2).

The *cerebrum,* or neomammalian brain, constitutes five-sixths of the human brain and makes language, operational thinking, analysis and planning ahead possible. This largest part of the brain is divided into two hemispheres that are connected by the largest band of neurons found in the brain, the *corpus callosum.* The left hemisphere generally processes things more in parts and sequentially and is more active when we experience positive emotions. The right hemisphere recognizes negative emotions, processes information more globally, and is more engaged in initial or novel experiences (Jensen, 1998, p. 8).

Covering the cerebrum is the *cortex,* or neocortex, which houses two-thirds of the neurons. It is within this thin layer composed of billions of columns of neurons that it is believed that genuine learning takes place (Weber, 1998). The brain is divided by scientists into lobes, each carrying out a variety of functions. It is currently believed that in the rear of the brain the *occipital* lobe is responsible for visual processing. The left and right *temporal* lobes are the location for speech and language, hearing, memory and meaning, and spatial information; the *frontal* lobes are the centers for planning, decision making, and creativity (figure 1.3).

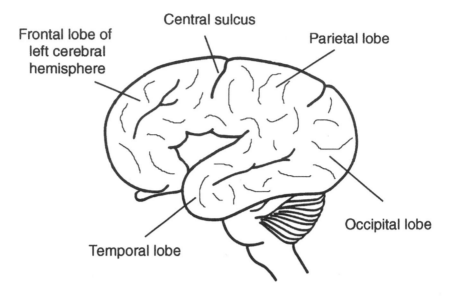

Central sulcus

Frontal lobe of left cerebral hemisphere

Parietal lobe

Temporal lobe

Occipital lobe

Figure 1.3 Lobes of the Brain

What we are learning about the physiology of the human brain and how it functions is expanding our understanding of why we have developed the capacity to learn, as well as how we learn. According to Robert Sylwester, animals (and humans) have brains because they can move and can travel to seek food, shelter, and mates and because they are capable of moving away from unfavorable conditions. Since we move, we need a cognitive system that can "comprehend and integrate sensory input and intelligently determine motor output" (unpublished).

Our survival as a social species and our ability to function in a wide variety of environments over a long life span are the result of our brain's adaptability. In order to thrive and survive as a species we needed to be able to rapidly evaluate our surroundings and quickly respond to the conditions that we encountered. As a result, humans developed many discrete skills over about a million years, and more recently (within the last 30,000–60,000 years) we have been able to combine these skills, create language and develop a broad intelligence and an increased capacity to learn (Abbott, 1997, p. 7).

Brain development during pregnancy, infancy and early childhood is critical and recent brain research supports the theories of Freud and Piaget in their assumptions that there are critical periods of development in the early years from birth to five. Most neuroscientists agree that the brain is not mature at birth and that significant development takes place postnatally. The fetal brain from the ninth week onward develops with incredible speed producing 250,00 neurons per minute (Wolfe, 1997). At birth our brains have the potential to assimilate a large variety of stimuli. Over time we develop mental routines and patterns in response to the stimuli we experience and we develop neural networks in response to our environment (Cardellichio and Field, 1997, p. 33). These neural networks or connections among the neurons are the system by which the neurons communicate as they collaborate to interpret stimuli and initiate responses. Those neural networks that are frequently used or stimulated by the environment are strengthened and their interconnectedness is increased through a process referred to as *neural branching*. Those neural networks not stimulated or infrequently used atrophy and cease to function, a process identified by scientists as *neural pruning*.

From birth to about age 5–6 the brain increases dramatically in size and is shaped by its environment and the experiences it encounters. In these early years, researchers have found, it is important that the brain is adequately stimulated through interactions with both people and the environment. According to Contine (1995), the brain creates inference frameworks from these early experiences and as "a rule of thumb the richer the child's environment, the greater the growth and development of the brain" (p. 14). Children with more highly developed brains (stronger and more interconnected neural networks) are more likely to have greater learning ability, higher levels of motivation, and accelerated readiness to begin school.

While there is a definite organization of the brain at birth related to our genetic programming for basic survival, our brains are also capable of changing their physical structure based on our experiences with the environment. The ability of neural networks to continue to generate and to modify themselves throughout life is referred to as *brain plasticity*.

The basic development of the brain is, according to Sylwester (1995), quite simple:

- Create an initial excess of cells and connections among the related areas of the brain.
- Strengthen over time the useful connections and eliminate those that are inefficient or unused.
- Maintain enough flexibility to allow neural networks to shift and change (p.117)

These physiological changes in the brain's architecture (branching, pruning, and plasticity) may in fact be the physical evidence that learning has taken place.

HOW WE LEARN

We now know that learning changes the brain as the brain rewires itself in response to new stimulation, experiences, and acquired behaviors, constructing for itself meaning and contrasting what is new with what it already thinks it knows. When something happens that we have experienced many times, it has no impact on us. We assimilate it into our existing mental frameworks. When something diverges from our past experience, we attempt to accommodate it, changing what we believe to fit the new event but also adapting the new event to fit what we believe we already know. While this view of learning is more prevalent today than in decades past, it is still not universally accepted. It conflicts with our educational traditions and our intellectual history (Bracey, 1994).

Dominant theories of learning have been based on what Marshall (1998) calls *false proxies,* such as seat time and coverage, which have substituted for indicators of genuine understanding. She writes,

As a result we created "brain antagonistic" learning environments that actually inhibit integrated thought, distort the learner's identity and competence, make pattern formulation and constructed meaning difficult and discourage skepticism, inventiveness, inquiry and complex cognition—the very skills and predisposition needed for the knowledge era (p. 48).

Departmentalization of curriculum, didactic instruction, prescribed knowledge, and competencies based on the accumulation of seat time and credits are all in conflict with what we are coming to understand about learning and the conditions necessary for it to take place efficiently.

All brain activity occurs spontaneously and automatically in response to experience. We do not need to be taught to learn. Challenge, interaction, and feedback appear to be the essentials of the teaching/learning process (Abbott, 1997, p. 8). Learning is most effective when it is active, goal directed, and personally relevant. Ron Brandt, in his book *Powerful Learning* (1998), delineates what he calls the principles of human learning, which he derives from his survey of cognitive psychology and brain research. They include:

- People learn what is meaningful to them.
- People learn more when they accept challenging but achievable goals.
- Learning is developmental.
- Individuals learn differently.
- Learning takes place through social interaction.
- People need feedback to learn.
- Successful learning involves the use of strategies that themselves are learned.
- A positive emotional climate influences learning.

These principles and those developed by other authorities in the field, such as Caine and Caine's (1991) Twelve Principles of the Mind (figure 1.4), can serve as a theoretical framework for creating brain-based methods, materials, and school environments that will capitalize on our growing understanding of how the mind works.

If learning is the direct result of the brain's associative properties and memory systems, then what we come to know is constructed by our brains through situational and experiential encounters and is influenced by pace, connectiveness, context, and prior understanding. Our minds are constantly searching for meaning through what Weber (1998) calls a "sociocognitive" process that involves social interaction, cognition, and language (p. 67). In short, we are discovering that genuine learning and teaching are far more complex than most educators had previously thought.

Twelve Principles of the Mind

1. The brain is a parallel processor.
2. Learning engages the entire physiology.
3. The search for meaning is innate.
4. The search for meaning occurs through patterning.
5. Emotions are critical to learning.
6. The brain processes parts and wholes simultaneously.
7. Learning involves both focused attention and peripheral perception.
8. Learning involves conscious and unconscious processes.
9. We have at least two memory systems.
10. We understand and remember best those things we learn in context.
11. Learning is enhanced by challenge and inhibited by threat.
12. Each learner's brain is unique.

Figure 1.4

The implications of these emerging theories of learning are significant for teachers, administrators, parents, and students. They suggest the need to change not only how we teach and assess learning but also how we organize what students need to learn as well as how classrooms and schools are organized and operate.

HOW SCHOOLS SHOULD BE ORGANIZED

The implications of the emerging theories on learning based on the revelations of neuroscience and the cognitive sciences are significant. Beyond affirming some of our common practices, they suggest the need for changes not only in how we teach and assess learning but also in how we organize the information students need to learn and how schools and the classrooms within them should operate.

Educational methods and practices have treated the brain as an empty and passive repository into which knowledge can be transmitted. Specialists in departmentalized or self-contained programs deliver discrete knowledge and specific skills through passive learning strategies in assembly line fashion. As a result we have created what Marshall (1998) calls "brain antagonistic learning environments," placing us on a collision course with what we are coming to understand about learning (p. 50). What may be needed in order for our schools and classrooms to be more compatible with the natural functioning of the brain are changes that bring greater:

- Coherence to the organization of the school day
- Relevance to the content of the curriculum
- Authenticity to the nature of the learning provided
- Collegiality between and among the students and adults within the school organization

Defining the changes that need to be made and how these changes can be made must be linked to what we now know and are currently learning about the brain and how it learns. Those changes will have to be implemented at the classroom level by enlightened teachers capable of rethinking every aspect of the educational process in terms of what they are doing and how they are getting things done.

For a classroom or school to be considered brain compatible it will need to be more personal and less isolated, free from risk, and involved in the intrapersonal and social development of the child along with the student's intellectual growth. Students will have to have increasing responsibility for their own mastery learning of a more relevant and personal, integrated curriculum. And they will have to be more actively engaged in complex cognitive experiences and authentic inquiry over extended periods of time. This will require a more flexible school schedule, alternatives to the traditional ways in which students are grouped, and an extension of learning opportunities that go beyond the traditional school campus and traditional school calendar (*Breaking Ranks,* 1996, p. 45)

It will also require a reshaping of the relationships among teachers and between teachers and administrators, as the adults in the organization attend to their own professional development and interactions in ways that model the new learning theory being applied to the classrooms. The very same conditions recommended for the brain-compatible classroom are applicable to the school as a brain-compatible workplace. Professional development, supervision of staff, and the administration of the school or school district should be as influenced by brain research as are the instruction, curriculum, classroom management, and assessment.

John Bruer (1998) suggests that "the challenge for educators is to develop learning environments and practices that can exploit the brain's lifelong plasticity . . . and constantly test the educational efficacy of these environments (p. 9)." It is equally important for both teachers and administrators to keep this mission in mind. Brain research is important because it validates what we do and can identify for us those things we should no longer do. It can help us teach the student to better understand her own thinking and on a personal level help us to understand how we think and learn and relate to others.

SUMMARY

This chapter summarized the knowledge explosion that is taking place in the cognitive sciences and neurosciences and the implications of this research for educational practice. Our growing understanding of the brain and how it functions will impact the mental models that have guided our teaching practices and our assumptions about how students learn. An overview of the physiology of the brain and how it works was provided as a basis for understanding the emerging theories of learning and the impact they will have on classroom practice and school organization. Some of the changes that will need to be made were briefly introduced, and the importance of brain research to teachers, students, and administrators was highlighted.

REFERENCES

Abbott, John. (March, 1997). "To be Intelligent." *Educational Leadership,* Alexandria, VA: Association for Supervision and Curriculum Development. 54 (6), 7.

————. (January, 1998). "Turning Learning Upside Down and Inside Out." *The School Administrator,* Arlington, VA: American Association of School Administrators. 55(1), 17–21.

Bracey, Gerald B. (1994). *Transforming America's Schools: An Rx for Getting Past Blame,* Arlington, VA: American Association of School Administrators, 39–41.

Brandt, Ron. (1998). *Powerful Learning*. Alexandria, VA: Association for Supervision and Curriculum Development, 12.

Breaking Ranks: Changing an American Institution, A Report of the National Association of Secondary School Principals on the High School of the 21st Century. (1996). Reston, VA: National Association of Secondary School Principals, 45.

Bruer, John T. (May, 1998). "Let's Put Brain Science on the Back Burner." *NASSP Bulletin,* Reston, VA: National Association of Secondary School Principals. 82 (598), 9.

Caine, Renate Nuemmella and Geoffrey Caine. (1991). *Making Connections: Teaching and the Human Brain.* Alexandria, VA: Association for Supervision and Curriculum Development, 180.

Cardellichio, Thomas and Wendy Field. (March, 1998), "Seven Strategies That Encourage Critical Thinking." *Educational Leadership,* Alexandria, VA: Association for Supervision and Curriculum Development. 54 (6), 33.

Contine, Tom. (1995). *Current Brain Research: Classroom Applications. "Brain Friendly Classrooms."* Kearny, NE: Educational Systems Associates, 14.

Goleman, Daniel. (1995). *Emotional Intelligence: Why It Can Matter More Than IQ.* New York: Bantam Books, 9–12.

Jensen, Eric. (1998). *Teaching with the Brain in Mind.* Alexandria, VA: Association for Supervision and Curriculum Development, 9–10.

Marshall, Stephanie Pace. (May, 1998). "Creating Pioneers for an Unknown Land: Education for the Future." *NASSP Bulletin,* Reston, VA: National Association of Secondary School Principals. 82 (598), 48–55.

Sylwester, Robert. (Unpublished). "Intelligence: What It Is, How to Enhance It."

———. (1995). *A Celebration of Neurons: An Educator's Guide to the Human Brain.* Alexandria, VA: Association for Supervision and Curriculum Development, 4.

———. (January, 1998). "The Brain Revolution." *The School Administrator,* Arlington, VA: American Association of School Administrators. 55 (1), 6–10.

Weber, Ellen. (May, 1998). "Marks of a Brain Based Assessment: A Practical Checklist." *NASSP Bulletin,* Reston, VA: National Association of Secondary School Principals. 82 (598), 63–72.

Wolf, Pat. (1997). "Translating Brain Research into Educational Practice." *Satellite Broadcast.* Alexandria, VA: Association for Supervision and Curriculum Development.

CHAPTER 2

Ready, Set, Learn

We ask students to identify objects of attention, to sustain attention and to ignore other stimuli in the environment. They can do this only when the learning is relevant, engaging and chosen by the learner. Otherwise it is a statistical improbability.

Eric Jensen

What we learn and remember are those bits of information, specific skills, and behaviors to which we pay attention. Our brain gathers information through the sensory receptors that comprise our senses. Our eyes, ears, nose, mouth, and skin are not in and of themselves intelligent. They are simply receiving a constant stream of sensory input about our bodies and the environment that surrounds us. Our sensory memories and our instincts for survival sort information and determine what is important. The brain is neither a sponge that absorbs everything we sense nor a camera that records and remembers everything we experience. In order to function efficiently, the brain must attempt to pay conscious attention to that which is important and to ignore in general the irrelevant. This unconscious process takes place in under a second by means of our sensory register. While our brain is always paying attention to something, what our brain considers irrelevant is gone (figure 2.1). Only what we pay attention to can be learned.

Our brain's ability to focus and maintain its attention on an object or event is critical to learning, and memory and attention are basic elements in classroom motivation and management. Our attention system is designed to quickly recognize and respond, but students must attend to subtle differences and gradual change. Teachers must therefore understand the

Information Processing

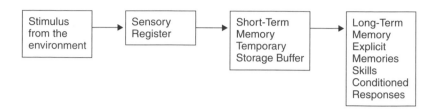

Figure 2.1

basic mechanisms and processes that regulate our attention if they are to make useful application of what we are learning from brain research.

GETTING THE BRAIN'S ATTENTION

In any effective system of attention, according to Robert Sylwester, we must identify and focus on what is important, sustain attention while monitoring related information and ignoring other stimuli, access memories that aren't active but may be relevant, and shift attention when important new information arrives. It begins as a passive process and quickly turns to active engagement. It is a constant, conscious selection of current focus that provides us with a short-term memory buffer that allows us to hold a few units of information for several minutes while we determine whether to go on to something else or store the data in our long-term memory (1995, p. 78).

Researchers working on how the brain makes its decision to pay attention believe that we are naturally drawn to those experiences that are related to our immediate needs or survival, that are:

- Personally meaningful to us
- Related to something we already know
- Novel, interesting, or exciting

We pay attention to those things that appear to be important to us and to initial experiences that appear to us to make sense (Wolfe, 1997).

A second factor in capturing our attention is our emotions. They influence very strongly what we choose to attend to. Understanding that connection between cognition and emotion, say Caine and Caine (January, 1998), opens us up to a whole new view of the teaching and learning process (p. 15). How students feel about a learning situation determines the amount of attention they will devote to it. Emotions, therefore, have a strong influence on how and what we learn. Students, for example, who feel physically safe and emotionally secure in the school and in the classroom are better able to focus on the content of what it is they are expected to learn. Creating a learning environment therefore that is emotionally conducive to learning is critically important. Sousa (December, 1998) believes that teaching students about their emotions and how to manage them is an area that also should be of growing interest to teachers (p. 35).

Educators need to be enlightened about how emotions influence our attention and affect our ability to learn. Emotions drive attention, and attention drives both learning and memory. We remember little content that we don't emotionally attach to. The emotional attachments we make relate to the learning experience and our relationships with others involved in the learning experience. These emotional connections are important between the teacher and the students, among the students themselves, and among the other adults in the organization. Teachers cannot create a positive emotional climate for their students unless the school has created a positive emotional climate for the teachers. According to Kovalik (1998), teachers cannot give to their students what they do not have for themselves (p. 29).

Daniel Goleman's 1995 book *Emotional Intelligence* summarized the breakthroughs in our understanding of the strong influence that emotions play in how we both develop and learn. A person's feelings about a learning situation determines the amount of attention that that person will devote to it. Emotions interact with reason to support or inhibit learning activities. According to Goleman (1995), students must feel physically safe and emotionally secure in their school and classroom before they can process the enormous amount of information we give them. Students must be encouraged to take risks and must have a strong sense that their teachers want to help them.

Teachers also must explore the why and how of teaching students about their emotions. Goleman suggests that we teach students how to control

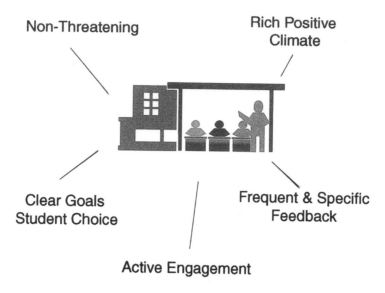

Non-Threatening   Rich Positive
                            Climate

Clear Goals   Frequent & Specific
Student Choice   Feedback

Active Engagement

The Ideal Classroom

Figure 2.2

their impulses, delay gratification, express their feelings, manage their relationships, and reduce their stress. Each of these skills contributes to improving the students' ability to pay attention and to concentrate on what it is they need to learn. Students should be taught to recognize that they can manage their emotions for greater productivity and that they can develop important interpersonal and intrapersonal skills for greater success in both their personal and professional lives (Sousa, 1998, p. 8).

While emotion energizes learning and memory, because those experiences associated with strong feelings are best remembered, prolonged high levels of emotion can result in undesirable levels of attention that may in fact inhibit learning. When the level of tension is high and prolonged, the brain's neural energy will be directed to reducing the source of the tension rather than to learning the task at hand. From a psychological point of view, therefore, the ideal classroom is neither emotion free nor emotionally supercharged but one in which a reasonable balance is struck between the two extremes (figure 2.2).

The attention spans of most students while engaged in a learning task are brief, usually ranging from three to seven minutes. During these short time spans the brain's level of neural energy remains high, allowing students to focus and concentrate intensely. These episodes quickly deplete the brain's store of neural energy. This reality of human biology, physiology, and neurology explains why the majority of children and teenagers are unable to remain attentive for long periods of time.

Like the body, the brain is able to exert itself intensely for short bursts of time, usually measured in minutes. These bursts are followed by periods in which the brain lapses into spans of inactivity and sometimes lethargy. With this depletion of energy, the brain loses the ability to focus and concentrate on learning tasks. To enable students to reengage and to focus at high levels, Contine (1995, p. 36) suggests that teachers consider changing topics, alternating instructional strategies, varying the level of student participation, using humor, and providing breaks (figure 2.3).

What we learn must be personally meaningful, challenging, and developmentally appropriate. How we learn must be in our own style, with choices and control, using what we already know, with opportunities for social interaction, helpful feedback, and the chance to acquire and use information about our emotions. Where we learn must be a pos-

Strategies for Sustaining Student Focus and Attention

- Shift the emphasis of concentration.
- Provide short rest breaks.
- Allow students to stand and stretch.
- Offer musical respites.
- Change the method of instruction from passive to active.
- Alternate covert and overt student learning behaviors.
- Inject elements of humor into the learning environment.
- Provide students with drinks or snacks.
- Allow students to socially interact. (Contine, 1995, p. 36)

Figure 2.3

itive emotional climate and a physical environment that supports the intended learning (Brandt, 1998, p. 12).

GETTING THE EMOTIONAL BRAIN'S ATTENTION

Our emotions guide us in facing predicaments and tasks too important to leave to our intellect alone, according to Goleman (1995, pp. 3–6). Instinctive reactions have become etched into our nervous systems over a long and critical period of biological evolution when these reactions made the difference between survival and death. The new realities of our modern civilization have risen with such rapidity that the slow march of evolution cannot catch up. All emotions in essence are an impulse to act, instant plans for handling life that evolution has instilled in us. Our initial emotional response to a situation, therefore, may not always be the most appropriate or productive course of action to take.

The root of the word *emotion* is *motere,* Latin for "to move." The prefix *e-* is added to connote "to move away." In our emotional repertoire, each of our emotions plays a unique role and is revealed in a distinctive biological signature (Goleman, 1995, pp. 3–6) (figure 2.4). These biological propensities to act are shaped further by our life experience and our culture.

The Physiology of Emotions

- Anger—blood flows to the hands, heart rate increases, rush of hormones
- Fear—blood flows to the large skeletal muscles, attention to the threat
- Happiness—inhibits negative feelings, fosters increased available energy
- Surprise—lifts eyebrows to take in a larger visual sweep
- Disgust—closes nostrils to noxious odors, spits out toxins
- Sadness—drop in energy and enthusiasm, stays close to home

Figure 2.4

The rational mind is the mode of comprehension we are typically conscious of, the part of the brain more prominent in awareness and the part of the brain that is thoughtful and reflective. Alongside this system of knowing is an impulsive and powerful, if sometimes illogical, emotional brain.

The term *emotional brain* is a convenient usage that combines a number of related brain functions; however, no single unified brain system regulates our emotions. Learning is a body-mind activity. These emotional systems developed for a variety of reasons, and many parts of the brain participate in our emotional life. Most often our emotional response is generated unconsciously and is something that happens to us rather than something we will to occur. Neurotransmitters in the brain responsible for synaptic leaps are but one form of the informational substances found throughout the body and brain that carry out the process of learning. Peptides and other chemicals in the body serve as informational substances produced in every cell in the body. The body and brain communicate constantly via these chemical messages that determine what is worth attending to and the attitude with which to attend. These chemical exchanges filter the input of our experiences and significantly alter our perceptions and the input selected and allowed in during any learning situation (Kovalik, 1998, p. 31).

Since we have weak conscious control over our emotions, they can flood our consciousness and provide powerful motivation for both positive and negative future behaviors (Le Doux, 1996). When we confront situations that have no sense of immediacy, a relatively slow pathway that uses the thalamus, hippocampus, and cerebral cortex circuitry allows us to reflect on and analyze the situation and to prepare a response. When, however, we confront a situation requiring a rapid reflex, the pathway of the thalamus, amygdala, and hippocampus directly activates the pituitary/adrenal gland circuitry, initiating a stress response that is designed to provide a short-term, high-energy (flight or fight) response to the perceived threat (Le Doux, 1996). This biologically driven response influences our ability to focus our neural energy on learning, in that mild intellectual challenge can enhance learning but excessive stress in the classroom can shift us into a mode of operation in which we react to the danger rather than thinking rationally about the situation.

Teaching students about the emotional brain can help students deal with each other in personal conflict and in handling their emotional responses. Strategies to deal with our emotions can be taught.

GETTING THE NOVEL BRAIN'S ATTENTION

In addition to understanding how the emotions affect a student's ability to pay attention to and concentrate on the things we want him to learn, educators need to come to grips with the fact that today's students are coming to school with a different, or novel, brain. From birth, even before birth, the human brain is shaped by and learns from its environment. Children today grow up in a very different environment than their teachers grew up in and an environment that is dramatically different than the environment that children grew up in only a decade ago. According to Sousa (1998), "The home environment of a child several decades ago was usually quiet. Parents and children did a lot of talking and reading. School therefore was a much more interesting place and because there were few distractions school was an important influence on a child's life" (p. 2).

Today's children, however, are growing up in a very different home environment shaped by a culture heavily influenced by multimedia and an ever-increasing pace of activity. These influences are changing what the developing brain is learning from the world. The novel brain of today's student is attentive to and will focus on sensory input that is rapid, emotional, pleasurable and of short duration. By comparison, school is seen as "dull, nonengaging and much less interesting than what is outside of school" (Sousa, 1998, p. 2). Educators can either decry the changing brain or adjust to accommodate these changes.

The brain, as discussed in chapter 1, literally customizes itself for a particular lifestyle (brain plasticity) and prunes away unused cells and neural connection (neural pruning). The experiences that students have before they begin to attend school and the experiences they have outside of school are critically important to shaping their abilities, the attitudes they have about school, and their motivation to learn.

Sylwester (1997) estimates that of the 150,000 hours students live between the ages of 1 and 18, they spend roughly one-third (50,000 hours) asleep and nearly two-thirds of the remaining 100,000 hours involved in solitary activities and in direct relationships with family and friends, activities that play a major role in the development and maintenance of important personal memories. Approximately only 35,000 hours are spent in the larger culture, and only 12,000 of those hours are spent in school. Almost twice as many hours are spent on activities and experiences outside the classroom.

To be competitive with the modern culture in which students spend the majority of their time, schools must create learning experiences that are as engaging, as interesting, as multisensory, and as meaningful as what the students experience outside the classroom.

SUSTAINING THE BRAIN'S ATTENTION

Sustaining the brain's attention, for example, focusing and concentrating, depends upon the amplification of relevant sensory information and the suppression of irrelevant sensory information. Students succeed academically, according to Jensen (1998, p. 43), when they have the ability to tune in like a radio to an exact, focused bandwidth and when they are provided with opportunities to "go internal" periodically in order to figure things out (Jensen, 1998, pp. 45–46). We all have attention cycles that have highs and lows. Blood flow and breathing actually change during these highs and lows, and those changes can alter the brain's chemistry and affect learning. The brain is simply not designed for continuous high-level attention, and the demand for constant attention in the teaching/learning process is actually counterproductive. In order to learn, the brain needs time to process new information, create meaning from that information, and store the new learning. As a result, in order to sustain students' attention, each new learning activity should be followed by short, divergent activities that allow the students to sort through what they have learned by:

- Discussing it with others
- Completing written exercises
- Generating their own questions
- Or proposing what-if scenarios

Factors That Influence Attention/Concentration

Student attention will be less than 10 minutes when . . .	Student attention can be up to as much as 90 minutes when . . .
the teacher requires, selects or directs the learning activity	the students select or direct the learning activity
the material is not relevant to the learner	the material is authentic and has personal meaning for the learner
the learner is not actively engaged	the learner is involved in active sensory engagement

Figure 2.5

Classrooms usually sacrifice the joy of learning for instructional efficiency, classroom management, or meeting timelines for educational outcomes, says Armstrong (1998, p. 35). When tedium rules, students divert their attention and concentration away from the lesson plan and take their curiosity inside. Learning becomes more effective and concentration is enhanced when students engage in activity that diminishes the influence of external stimuli and amplifies those things on which we want them to focus (figure 2.5).

Minilectures, group work, time for reflection, individual work, and team project time are all useful strategies to aid students in maintaining their focus. Even simple variations of the routine, such as teacher location in the room, or a change in voice volume or tone can extend the attentional bias. But like getting the brain's attention, sustaining the brain's attention is a balance between the introduction of novelty and the brain's affinity for ritual and predictable structure.

DOWNSHIFTING

As we have seen, our brains are attentive and focused and able to learn when we are challenged and interested. We are unable to learn when we feel threatened or have a feeling of helplessness. This narrowing of the brain's receptivity is referred to as *downshifting,* a term borrowed from Les Hart (Caine and Caine, May, 1998, p. 5). It is a psychophysiological response associated with helplessness or fatigue. When our brains downshift we are unable to objectively evaluate information or access all we know and are less able to engage in complex intellectual tasks or form memories. It is a phenomenon that can prevent us from learning and from engaging in complex intellectual tasks. Simply put, when we perceive a threat, the more primitive and emotional parts of our brain begin to dominate.

A threat is anything that triggers a sense of helplessness, and what may constitute a threat varies from person to person. Children's lives are filled with threats. Poverty, malnourishment, child abuse, and family and community violence can all leave a child with a sense of helplessness. But the way in which a classroom is managed and the nuances of the classroom climate can also present psychological or emotional threats to which the child's body's physical response is identical.

Traditional classroom pedagogy can be a threat when the teacher is seen as controlling what is taught, when it is taught, and how the learning will be assessed. A typical day for students can be filled with stressful situations related to their classroom status, their expectations and disappointments, and the degree to which their predictions about themselves and others match the reality of what transpires. At the moment the students detect a situation they see as stressful, the brain begins to activate its mechanisms for defense and behaviors that are great for survival but lousy for learning. Teachers who want to obtain their students' attention and maintain their concentration must be prepared to manage conditions in the classroom that can reduce threats and to teach students how to mediate and release their stress.

There is a set of conditions that tend to induce downshifting in the classroom. They include when:

- Prescribed correct outcomes have been established
- Personal meaning is limited
- Rewards and punishments are externally controlled
- Restrictive timelines are given
- Work is unfamiliar and little support is available (Caine and Caine, 1998, p. 6)

The human brain has a finite supply of neural energy, and whenever that energy is diverted away from learning tasks in order to handle stress,

threat, anxiety, or embarrassment, the probability of learning is dimin-
ished. Students can feel threatened when:

- Asked to believe or accept something that conflicts with prior,
  closely held beliefs
- Behavior of another person is perceived as physically, emotionally,
  or psychologically harmful or potentially harmful
- Personal or familial beliefs about right or wrong are questioned,
  challenged, or threatened
- They sense stress or a threat or are embarrassed (Contine, 1995, p. 24)

We cannot attend, focus, or learn without purpose or meaning or in a
high-threat environment.

Some degree of concern is a necessary variable in motivation or our
willingness to attend and devote energy to learning something new. On
the one hand, if we have no concern about a particular learning, there is
little chance we will learn it. On the other hand, when we recognize a
need to acquire information or a skill, a moderate concern or stress
results, and that level of emotion heightens our attentiveness and ability
to remain focused. Of course if the stress becomes too much, downshifting occurs and we go past the optimum level and shift our focus to
the emotions generated by the stress, and our ability to concentrate on
the learning fades (Sousa, 1998, p. 8) (figure 2.6.).

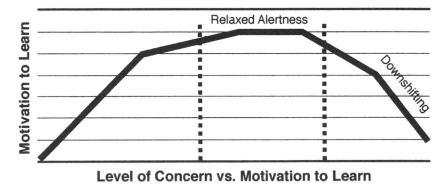

Figure 2.6

Emotions are a double-edged sword. Too little emotion produces no effect, but too much emotion, and the brain shuts down. The affective side of learning is the critical interplay between how we feel, act, and think, and our emotions are a critical source of information. Teachers who help their students feel good about themselves and learning through classroom success and friendships are doing the very things a student's brain craves. We cannot teach and students will not learn unless the important role of emotions is acknowledged and integrated into the daily operation of teaching. That means a classroom with high challenge and low stress and a state of "relaxed alertness" for the student.

IMPLICATIONS FOR A BRAIN-FRIENDLY CLASSROOM

If how a person feels about a learning situation determines the amount of attention he or she will devote to it, then what should teachers do to increase the probability that they are creating a learning environment that is addressing a student's natural, emotional, and novel attention-triggering mechanisms?

To address the natural attention-triggering mechanisms of the brain, Carol Cummings (1990) suggests that getting the students' attention involves the creation of a mental set. Since students come to the classroom with a wealth of information, a learning history, and experiences, it is important to connect with that information and bring it forward to the new learning in a positive way. In defining the mental set, Cummings encourages teachers to answer for themselves three questions when initiating a new learning:

- How can I capture the learner's attention?—Something novel or different that might capture the students' initial interest and focus.
- How can I provide meaning for the lesson by association and organization and hold the students' attention?—Eliminate having the students wondering what the lesson is about by establishing logical relationships between the new information and what they already know, thereby giving the students an organization for the new learning and extending their curiosity.
- How can I involve the learners in the learning and cause them to devote energy to learning the new information?—By actively engag-

ing in the learning and amplifying its focus and suppressing the stimuli that might refocus the students' attention (p. 161).

Developing a creative lesson introduction focuses the class on the highlights of the learning, sets the stage for the learning activity, and shapes the students' attitude towards the lesson. Building a bridge between the new information and what the students may already know directs the students' attention to the relevant information and can help focus the instructional behaviors.

When students understand the lesson objective and the teacher's expectations, student attention and focus are increased. Guesswork is eliminated. Students are given a sense of direction and security and a framework for evaluating their personal progress and success.

Beyond the instructional strategy, others suggest that teachers need to pay close attention to the emotional climate they create in their classrooms and lessons. Kovalik (1998) writes of the importance of the emotional triggers that influence attention (pp. 33–34). A classroom must be absent of threats if it is to be a place where students can attend to learning. This involves building a sense of community and the frequent use of collaborative activities. Students must experience an environment characterized by trustworthiness, truthfulness, and active listening, a place where put-downs are prohibited and each student is encouraged to do his or her personal best. Classrooms that have clear expectations for all behaviors that are consistently applied have proven to be the most conducive to student learning.

Extrinsic rewards such as tokens, gimmicks, and coupons no longer make sense when compared with more attractive alternatives to capturing and holding a student's attention. Extrinsic rewards have been studied and rejected as a motivating strategy and may actually damage the student's natural intrinsic motivation to learn. Five key strategies, according to Jensen (1998), help students to tap into this natural curiosity (figure 2.7) (p. 68).

Students' attention and their motivation to learn is influenced by a range of factors, including a well-organized and appropriately decorated classroom in which students regularly engage in complex learning activities that require problem solving and creative thinking. It is a classroom in which students are given some control over the selec-

Principles of the Brain-Friendly Classroom:
Gaining and Holding Student Attention

Eliminate Threat
uncover problems
avoid demands
manage behaviors

Actively Engage Emotions
use dreams, music, art
celebrate student success
win/win competitions

Create a Positive Climate
build relationships
use rituals/routines
use acknowledgments
enrich the learning
environment

Increase Feedback
peer evaluation
self-evaluation
computer programs
make feedback
timely and concise

Set Goals
establish meaning
provide choice
enunciate a clear purpose

Figure 2.7

tion of the learning activities and where opportunities for them to share their feelings are provided. Student opinions are valued in the brain-friendly classroom and students are encouraged to take risks. Academic competition is meaningful and academic cooperation is maximized (Contine, 1995, p. 25). Emotionally, students feel good and believe in their potential for academic success. Physically, the room is inviting and the distractions from learning are properly managed.

An additional variable in the attempt to capture and hold the students' attention may be movement. The cerebellum, which is believed to control our movement, takes up one-tenth of the brain's volume and contains about half of all its neurons. In the past it was believed that the cerebellum merely processed signals from the cerebrum to the motor cortex, but more recent research indicates a strong link between movement and thinking. The strong links that are being established between the cerebellum and memory, spatial perception, language, attention, emotion, nonverbal communication, and even decision making indicate that physical exercise, movement, and games can boost cognition (Jensen, 1998, p. 83).

In the same way that exercise shapes the muscles, heart, lungs, and bones, it is now believed that it also strengthens the key areas of the brain. Exercise or movement during learning fuels the brain with oxygen and feeds the brain neurotropens (high-nutrient foods), which enhance neural activity (Jensen, 1998, pp. 55–86). When movement is incorporated into a lesson, students are provided with the opportunity to physically enhance their attention mechanisms; and because exercise can reduce stress, there is a huge fringe benefit regarding the students' emotional attention as well. Brain-compatible learning means that teachers should weave physical activity and movement into their lessons, or even provide exercise breaks, for simple stretching is a means of gaining and sustaining student attention.

The brain-friendly classroom creates a synergy that makes it easier for students to focus and concentrate by making learning a whole-body experience that involves the cognitive, emotional, physical, and social attributes of the students' minds. It is a classroom where the information to be learned is delivered through multimodalities, engages the learner in social interaction, and is emotionally stimulating. The brain-friendly classroom provides time for reflection and a variety of activities and assessment opportunities from which students can choose.

SUMMARY

In this chapter we reviewed the physiology of the brain that relates to capturing students' attention and sustaining their focus on the learning activity. The brain has a number of attention triggers that are influenced by evolution, our emotions, and the environment in which we live. Together they dictate what we pay attention to and how much energy we will devote to acquiring new information or skills. Using this information to design a brain-friendly classroom in which students will be able to attend is not easy. A fine balance must be maintained between novelty and routine and the amount of stress or concern that students feel. It may be different for every student. The probability is that learning will take place in classrooms where the substance of the lesson is meaningful and relevant.

REFERENCES

Armstrong, Thomas. (1998). *Awakening Genius in the Classroom*. Alexandria, VA: Association for Supervision and Curriculum Development, 35.

Brandt, Ron. (1998). *Powerful Learning*. Alexandria, VA: Association for Supervision and Curriculum Development, 12.

Caine, Renate Nuemmella and Geoffrey Caine. (January, 1998). "How to Think About the Brain." *The School Administrator,* Arlington, VA: American Association of School Administrators. 55 (1), 12–16.

―――. (May, 1998). "Building a Bridge Between the Neurosciences and Education: Cautions and Possibilities." *NASSP Bulletin,* Reston, VA: National Association of Secondary School Principals. 82 (598), 1–8.

Contine, Tom. (1995). *Current Brain Research: Classroom Applications. "Brain Friendly Classrooms."* Kearny, NE: Educational Systems Associates, 24–36.

Cummings, Carol. (1990). *Managing a Cooperative Classroom: A Practical Guide for Teachers*. Edmonds, WA: Teaching Incorporated.

Goleman, Daniel. (1995). *Emotional Intelligence: Why It Can Matter More Than IQ*. New York: Bantam Books, 3–6.

Jensen, Eric (1998). *Teaching with the Brain in Mind*. Alexandria, VA: Association for Supervision and Curriculum Development, 17–86.

Kovalik, Susan and Karen Olsen. (May, 1998). "How Emotions Run Us, Our Students and Our Classrooms." *NASSP Bulletin,* Reston VA: National Association of Secondary School Principals. 82 (598), 29–37.

Le Doux, Joseph. (1996). *The Emotional Brain: The Mysterious Underpinnings of Emotional Life*. New York: Simon and Schuster.

Sylwester, Robert. (1995). *A Celebration of Neurons: An Educator's Guide to the Human Brain*. Alexandria, VA: Association for Supervision and Curriculum Development, 78.

―――. (Summer, 1997). "Bioelectronic Learning: The Effects of Electronic Media on the Developing Brain." *Tecnos.* 6 (2), 19–22.

Sousa, David. (1998). *Learning Manual for How the Brain Works*. Thousand Oaks, CA: Corwin Press, 2–8.

————. (December, 1998). "Is the Fuss about Brain Research Justified?" *Education Week,* 35, 52.

Wolfe, Pat. (1997). "Translating Brain Research into Educational Practice." Satellite Broadcast. Alexandria, VA: Association for Supervision and Curriculum Development.

CHAPTER 3

Memory, Meaning, and Deeper Understanding

Teachers who require students to recall large amounts of factual information from texts or lectures are at best developing self-discipline and at worst discouraged learners who feel incompetent.

Eric Jensen

Getting the learner's attention is important because paying attention is the first important step in the process of learning. But gaining a student's attention, in and of itself, is not enough to ensure that learning will take place. Learning is a process of paying attention to specific stimuli, processing that stimuli, and then storing that information and/or our response to it so that it can be recalled for future use. Learning is a process of creating memories and retaining information and skills.

Neuroscientists are not really certain where our memories are stored. Most believe that our memories are not localized in any one specific area but exist throughout the brain. What they are beginning to understand with increasing clarity is how our memories are created and the underlying physiology of how they are stored. Our senses stimulate our brains and continually bombard them with impressions as we see, hear, touch, taste, and smell. Most of these sensory experiences are held in our memory only briefly and then quickly vanish from our conscious awareness. Sometimes called the *sensory register,* our brain instantaneously sorts and analyzes these stimuli to make conscious and unconscious judgements about their value in a matter of seconds. We discard information we find useless and send on the rest for further analysis and processing.

How Memories are Created

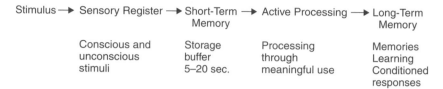

Stimulus ➞ Sensory Register ➞ Short-Term ➞ Active Processing ➞ Long-Term
                                Memory   Memory

Conscious and   Storage   Processing   Memories
unconscious   buffer   through   Learning
stimuli   5–20 sec.   meaningful use   Conditioned
                                                      responses

Figure 3.1

This information that is "saved" is held for perhaps five to twenty additional seconds in a "buffer," or short-term memory, where it is analyzed or processed in terms of its meaning to us, its connection to what we may already know, and its emotional context (Wolfe, 1997). If it is judged useless it is discarded and disappears from our memory. If it is perceived as valuable it is actively processed further and becomes a component of the brain's long-term, or permanent, memory system, where it will reside for the remainder of the brain's life (figure 3.1).

Brain imaging technology can now clearly identify the brain areas that are active when we try to remember or respond to something. At the cellular level scientists have discovered that when we "learn," something physical occurs in the synapses of the neural networks that process the information or skills that comprise the memory. The neural network is strengthened and the neural connections that constitute the network of neurons are permanently altered. We remember things that our brain determines are emotionally charged or likely to occur again in the future (Sylwester, 1995, p. 87). It takes less input and energy to trigger a strong memory (one with many relevant connections to related neural networks) and considerably more input and energy to recall a weak one.

For something to be learned or remembered, the brain must create a neural representation of the information, skill, event, or object that can be recalled. Our ability to cause these neural representations to be created depends on both our understanding and the learner's understanding of brain functioning and can be enhanced by the development of learning activities that will create multiple and interrelated neural networks that will make what we learn more accessible and powerful.

WORKING MEMORY/SHORT-TERM MEMORY

Different parts of the brain interact to preserve the meaningful experiences that constitute what we remember and what we learn. Biologists are decoding the underlying chemical process of neural networking, and neuroscientists are discovering how age, stress, and other factors affect the ways in which our brains remember. To scientists who study the brain, the wonder is that we retain as much as we do. Harvard psychologist Daniel Schacter observes, in his 1996 book, *Searching for Memory,* that the simple act of meeting a friend for lunch requires a vast store of memory. To do so requires a compendium of words, sounds, and grammatical rules; a record of the friend's appearance and manner; a catalog of restaurants; a mental map to get you there; and so on (p. 50).

To perform such tasks and to cope with the infinitely more complicated mental processes we tend to engage in, the brain maintains two separate types of memory systems:

- Working memory, or short-term memory, for juggling information in the present
- Permanent memory, or long-term memory, for storing information over extended periods of time

Contrary to popular opinion, our brains do not record everything that happens to us. Most of what we experience hovers briefly in our working memory, and, unless we are caused to do something to permanently store it, the experience, event, information, skill, or object will not be recorded or available for future recall. Working memory enables us to perform simple calculations or retain a phone number long enough to dial it. We can analyze and invent things in our working memory without creating a lasting record or altering the neural networks that comprise what we already know and can recall.

Working memory is the initial memory buffer that allows us to hold a few units of information (five to nine) that we are attending to for a short period of time while we determine their importance to us. Irrelevant information is discarded and other information is handled and forgotten about, according to Sylwester (1995, p. 92). Other information is set aside and handled later, some is stored, and some is incorporated into the neural networks, which represent what the brain remembers and knows and the procedures it has learned.

Working memory appears to function through temporary synchronized firing patterns that emerge between related networks in the thalamus (the current situation) and the cortex (related memories). The brain monitors the total sensory field and simultaneously searches for and focuses on the familiar, the interesting, and the important elements (Sylwester, 1995, p. 92). Since the working memory is limited to an average of seven units of information, we can learn to combine, or *chunk,* related bits of information into larger units so that more complex information can be manipulated in the working memory before a decision is made on what information ought to be stored.

Students should be taught to develop their short-term memory capabilities through activities that require them to analyze complex information and briefly hold key points in their memory. Making information too user friendly, however, by highly organizing it may not be the best strategy in all instances. The challenge of separating information into the relevant and irrelevant ideas associated with a particular learning allows the students to improve their analytical skills and to make associations and constructed meanings for themselves related to the new information being learned. This process may be critical in establishing the information's permanent storage and the students ability to recall it.

All incoming sensory data is filtered through the limbic system, which is the center for our emotional responses to incoming stimuli (Wolfe, 1997). As discussed in chapter 2, the decision to pay attention is based on the impulses generated by this primitive and emotional part of our brain. Information must have meaning or an emotional connection to be learned. Our emotions, therefore, are an essential element not only in determining what we attend to but also in influencing our ability to retain and recall what has been learned. Those experiences we have in our memory can be recalled either through their associative connection to what we already know or through their emotional context.

Emotions influence what we remember. Students who are anxious, angry, or depressed simply cannot learn. When emotions overwhelm our concentration, what is being swamped, according to Goleman (1995), is the short-term, or working, memory and what is interfered with is the ability to hold in our mind all the relevant information of the task at hand (pp. 28–29).

Working memory can retain information as simple as a phone number or as intricate as the plot of a play. It serves as an executive function that makes all other intellectual efforts possible, from speaking to problem solving. Sousa (1998) writes that studies show that what a person recalls from a learning episode is greatly influenced by that person's emotional state (p. 35). An uncomfortable feeling will make it easier to recall an unpleasant experience, and more pleasant feelings will make it easier to recall positive experiences. These findings reaffirm how important it is for the teacher to establish a positive emotional climate in the classroom.

LONG-TERM MEMORY

Our long-term memory records selected experiences and information in the outer layers of the brain for future use or recall through a network of neurons that communicate by relaying the chemical and electrical impulses that determine our responses to external and internal stimuli. Every time we perceive a sight, a sound, or an idea, a unique set of neurons is activated and sometimes altered by the new experience or information, and we learn. What we choose to store in our long-term memories may strengthen existing neural connections (relating to what we already know) or cause the network to become more dense or interconnected (as new associations are made between what we know and the new information). According to Dr. Barry Gordon of the Johns Hopkins School of Medicine, our memories, which include declarative knowledge, emotional experiences, behavioral responses, and reflexive and procedural skills, are actually, patterns of connections among neural cells (Cowley and Underwood, 1998, p. 51).

Memories involve thousands of neurons spanning the entire cortex. If they are not used, they will quickly fade. Memories that are activated repeatedly are embedded more deeply in our brains. The neurological networks are strengthened through frequent use. We can include things in our long-term memory simply by rehearsing them, but the decision to store something rarely involves purely conscious thought. The hippocampus, a small seahorse-shaped structure located in the center of the brain, is believed by many neuroscientists to be the deciding factor as to what we remember. It chooses to remember things that either have an emotional significance or are related to what we already know (Cowley and Underwood, p. 51).

If the hippocampus marks something for storage, it will lodge more easily among the things already linked within the cortex. Past experience, therefore, determines what new information is captured. Students, because of their different experiences, take away different information and learning from similar educational experiences.

Memories can be classified into distinctive categories that represent what we know, what we have experienced, what we have learned to do, and how we respond to given situations (figure 3.2). Our ability to create and recall these distinctive memories can be made more efficient and effective by carefully orchestrating the original learning episode or experience in which they are created.

Memories that relate to what we know and/or experience are called *declarative* memories and can be divided into two types, episodic and semantic memories. *Episodic* declarative memories are very personal and linked to a specific episode or context (an experience); *semantic* declarative memories are more abstract and context free and are often represented by symbols such as those used for language and mathematics (things we know). A third category of memories relates to automatic skills. Referred to as *procedural* memories, these learned and instinctual responses do not rely on conscious verbal recall except as a means to initiate, monitor, and stop the motor response (Sylwester, 1995, p. 93).

Our brains are most efficient at recalling and using episodic memories that have important personal meaning. They are much less efficient at mastering the important context-free semantic and procedural memories that constitute much of what we are expected to learn in school. These types of learned memories are the most difficult to master and, with respect to procedural memories, once learned are the hardest to forget. Memories not associated with an emotional context or personal meaning are best developed through observation of models, frequent practice, and continual feedback. That is why hands-on classroom experiences may be the most memorable. A physical process is highly likely to be recalled (Jensen, 1998, p. 108).

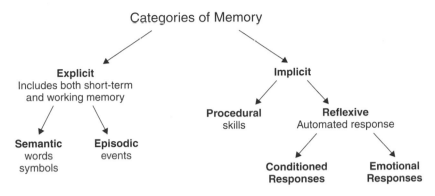

Figure 3.2

MEMORY AND RECALL

Memory and recall are critical to the learning process. Memories and what we learn are recorded as persistent changes in our brains. Our ability to remember is not located in a single part of the brain. Multiple memory locations and systems, according to Jensen (1998), are responsible for our best learning and recall (p. 99). Remembering and having the ability to recall what we know and what we have experienced is a process and not a specific skill.

Scientists believe that memories are formed by a rapid alteration of the synaptic connections. A specific protein molecule signals the nerve cells either to store a memory short term in our working memory or to engrave it permanently in long-term memory. The ability to recall the memory is determined by the way it is stored and the kinds of retrieval process that is needed to activate it. Factors that influence this storage-and-retrieval process range from the learner's body chemistry at the time the memory is formed to the nature of the learning experience and the extent to which the learner is actively and emotionally engaged in the teaching/learning process.

Memories are not retrieved like computer files but appear to be reconstructed when they are needed. There are several competing theories on how this might happen, but neuroscientists seem to agree that at the root of the retrieval process is a variety of neural pathways that are used for different types of memory recall (Jensen, 1998, p. 102). There appears to be no connection between how well a person thinks and how well the person remembers. We can retrieve, theoretically, almost anything we have paid attention to, but the success of retrieval or recall is dependent on the quality of the original learning and the context or meaning of the learning experience. Our ability to recall something may depend on which pathway we attempt to access.

Storage and retrieval of semantic declarative memories require the use of a symbolic stimulus. The ability to remember and recall semantic memories may be a relatively new and unnatural human skill. Until recent history, humans had little use for semantic recall, and it remains our weakest retrieval system (Jensen, 1998, p. 104). To create a semantic memory, the content of the learning must be meaningful, relevant, and organized and include sufficient sensory stimulation. We remember things that are new, the first and last things we see and hear, and those things that are different or unique from those things we know and experience. As Jensen (1998) writes, "Teachers who require students to recall large amounts of factual information from texts or lectures are at best developing self-discipline and at worse discouraged learners who feel incompetent" (p. 105).

Episodic declarative memories involve a contextual recall process. They are formed quickly and are easily updated. They require no drill and practice and are a natural and effortless process that is used by all of us. A smell, a sight, a sound, a physical sensation, or an emotional feeling can trigger an episodic memory. But episodic recall is not very accurate. These memories are created by pulling together information from different parts of the brain. As similar experiences are combined they may contaminate the specific information or experience we are trying to remember. We may even create a memory to compensate for missing information (Wolfe, 1997).

Procedural memories are our motor memories, or habit memories, and determine how we perform an acquired skill or respond behaviorally to specific stimuli. These skill memories are not easily acquired, but once learned, they are difficult to change or forget. To the brain, the body is not a separate entity but part of the same contiguous organism. What happens to the body, happens to the brain. Procedural memories involve the mastery of automatic skill sequences. These skill sequences, which direct our physical responses, are processed principally in the motor cortex and the cerebellum (Sylwester, unpublished). We appear to have adapted the skill-sequencing efficiency of procedural memory, according to Sylwester (1995, p. 98), to our need to recall combinations and sequences of facts that form a semantic memory. Storytelling, songs, games, metaphors, and related patterns of data organization provide a logical sequence for recalling information not unlike the automated sequences of skill performance.

THE IMPORTANCE OF MEANING

Meaning has a great impact on whether experiences, information, or skills will be learned and stored. Our past experiences and what we already know influence our ability to learn something new. They provide a filter that helps us attend to those things that have relevance to us and allow us to determine those experiences and new information that we can afford to discard. Teachers need to work harder at helping students to establish meaning for themselves, to make connections between subject areas, and to see the future use of what they are learning (Sousa, January, 1998, p. 24).

The brain responds differently to what it considers to be meaningless or meaningful information. One of the most important variables in the learning process is the establishment of meaning. This search for meaning is automatic, survival oriented, and basic to the human brain. "We are driven," write Caine and Caine (1991), "to make sense of the unfamiliar and incomplete stimuli. This search for meaning is at the heart of intrinsic motivation" (p. 91). A central point of Piaget's work was that children are always engaged in the process of making sense of things. Based on their synthesis of the current research, Caine and Caine (May, 1998) have identified three critical elements in establishing meaning for the learner:

- The state of mind of the learner must be characterized by low threat and high challenge.
- The learner must be immersed in a complex experience.
- The learner must actively process that experience (p. 3)

The brain is motivated to search for meaning and is most successful in establishing meaningful patterns and making connections when it is sufficiently challenged and free from threat. Novelty, purpose, and meaning are what cause the neurons to attend to an experience, to make connections among neural networks, and to form new patterns that cause us to adopt new ways of thinking and behaving. Our brain is a conceptualizer, a pattern seeker in search of the definitive elements of a remembered experience.

The brain is innately driven to search for meaning as it attempts to organize and make sense of everything within its surroundings. It resists the imposition of meaningless information and rejects isolated, discrete pieces of information that are unrelated to anything the individual has previously experienced. When students are able to give meaning to new information by relating it to what they already know or have experienced, the brain creates new frames of reference. New information acquires meaning, according to Contine (1995), when the student recognizes its relevance to some personal interest or need or when it is:

- Related to the student in a personal way
- Connected or linked to some prior learning
- Connected or linked to some prior experience (p. 16)

Establishing meaning in the avalanche of information that typically constitutes the school day can cause the learner to tune out. Teachers must therefore purposely focus more on the quality of the information we want students to learn and become less concerned with covering vast quantities of information that may be meaningless to the learner. When we find something meaningful, our brains are more active (Jensen, 1998, pp. 90–91).

There are two kinds of meaning: *reference meaning,* which is knowing what something is, and *sense meaning,* which is having experience with something. Relevance, emotion, and context or patterning enhance meaning, according to Jensen (1998), and all meaningful information or experiences have at least one of those three ingredients (pp. 92–93). Relevance causes a greater number of neurological connections and associations to be made among neurons. The more connections that are made, the more firmly new information is woven into the fabric of our long-term memory. Giving students time to link new information with prior learning and establishing meaning for themselves through social interaction with other students or through activities that guide the students towards making connections will enhance both understanding and retention.

Emotions can also enhance meaning. Emotions trigger brain chemicals that signal to the brain that something is important, and in this respect, emotion and meaning are linked. The emotional state of the learner, as we have seen, is important in getting the learner's attention and is equally important in determining what the student will remember. The emotional state is an important condition around which the teacher must orchestrate the learning. Instead of treating the cognitive substance of the information to be learned as separate and apart from its emotional context, a student's ability to understand and remember cognitive material can actually be enhanced when the learner has an emotional stake in the learning activity. Students need to express their emotions about a learning experience and have the opportunity to collaborate and share with other students what they are feeling and what they are learning.

The third ingredient of meaning is patterning or context. Patterning information means organizing and associating new information with previously developed mental hooks. The brain looks for and attempts to create patterns or context within which something can be understood. This desire to form meaningful patterns is innate, and again, according to Jensen (1998), many researchers believe that neurons exhibit learning only in groups (pp. 95–96). An infant as young as ten months old is drawn to and can recognize patterns more quickly than nonpatterns. The making of familiar connections (relevance) and locating neural networks (patterns or context) may be central to the formation of meaning. This natural tendency is the underlying power behind interdisciplinary curriculums and thematic instruction.

Increasing student retention and understanding of a new meaning is greatly enhanced when we address all three ingredients. Figure 3.3 lists several suggestions for increasing meaning in the classroom, although ultimately the learner must construct the meaning for himself or herself.

Suggestions for Teaching for Meaning

Visual organizers   Answering "why" questions

Pointing out patterns   Teaching taxonomies

Identifying relationships   Providing overviews

Identifying main ideas   Explaining future use

Allowing time for student processing

Figure 3.3

DEEPER UNDERSTANDING

Caine and Caine (1991) believe that what we have in education is an overemphasis on surface knowledge, "content devoid of significance to the learner," and that what is needed is the expansion of natural knowledge (p. 91). Surface knowledge has little meaning or connectiveness with other knowledge or with the social, emotional, or other aspects of the learner's psyche. Meaning, if it is to be evidence of deeper understanding and of longer-lasting retention, must be "felt" meaning, or insight, the coming together of parts in a way that creates a new whole—the AHA! Our deeper understanding of something stems from our sense of what is meant and how we can use the new information or experience in the future. Both meaning and use are indispensable to the acquisition of natural knowledge (Caine and Caine, 1991, p. 91). Because this deeper understanding varies from person to person, students can be assisted in acquiring deeper meaning by being given choices and by being given permission to explore their personal need to understand.

In practice, deeper meaning is acquired by increasing the quality and interconnections in the brain. The deeper we understand something, the more efficiently we form patterns or natural categories called *schemata* (Caine and Caine, 1991, p. 95). Experts are those individuals who have a natural knowledge or deeper understanding of a particular field. They have translated the elements of what they know into their own natural categories, and new information and experience within their area of expertise easily fall into place. Experts form larger patterns of neural networking that change the way they grasp both content and context as well as the ways in which they remember and recall what they know.

This deeper understanding, or natural knowledge, should be the objective of the educational process. While students need to grasp the formal operations that are necessary for abstract thinking, they must also be taught to be sensitive to the larger issues inherent in all content. Our goal should be to have students not only able to carry out procedures and remember discrete information but also able to understand the core concepts and key ideas that underlie what they are doing and what they need to understand.

If we expect students to find natural knowledge and deeper understanding, the curriculum must contain connections to their past experiences. Relevant connections must be made between and among subjects. The integration of the curriculum increases the students' understanding and retention, especially when students recognize how they will use their learning in the future.

THE IMPORTANCE OF PROCESSING TIME

Constructing meaning, deeper understanding, and longer retention requires the brain to go internal in order to figure things out. Our brains are not designed for continuous high-level attention or constant cognition. To expect constant attention in the classroom may be counterproductive to producing meaning, memory, and deeper understanding. Much of what we expect students to learn cannot be processed consciously, and new learning may require short, divergent activities that allow the students to create new meaning for themselves and to store that information in ways in which it can be readily recalled. Constant external input conflicts with the internal process of the students' construction of meaning from what they have just learned (Jensen, 1998, pp. 45–46).

It takes roughly six hours for a new skill to be consolidated and tagged for long-term storage (Sousa, 1998, p. 28). According to Sousa (1998) those who try to learn a second task before the first one is fully processed will have trouble learning either well. The presence of the first skill in working memory makes it harder to learn the second skill, whereas the second skill dilutes the memory of the first. The more similar the two skills are, the greater is the likelihood of confusion. New learning should be followed with discussions in small groups or other activities that guide the students in sorting out what they have just learned. Discussions, short writing assignments, and generating questions or what-if scenarios all encourage personal processing time. Jensen (1998) warns that "cramming more content per minute or moving from one piece of learning to the next virtually guarantees that little will be learned" (p. 47).

Timing, in fact, may be everything when it comes to learning. We tend to remember best those things that come first and last in a learning episode, and our percentage of remembering actually increases as the length of a learning activity decreases (Sousa, January 1998, p. 25). Therefore, not only *what* is presented but when a teacher presents information or a skill can be a major factor in determining how much a student remembers (figure 3.4). Shorter learning episodes are usually more effective. Lesson segments of twenty minutes are the most likely to hold a student's interest and result in the greatest retention. Students also need to rest, according to Sousa (1998). Although most teachers believe that staying on task throughout the learning period is best, current research seems to indicate that neurons need some downtime to consolidate information. We are more likely to keep students focused during the lesson segments if we go off task between segments (p. 42). Even rest times allow the brain to recycle. When we shut down the external stimuli, the brain can concentrate on linking new information to existing associations, uses, and procedures.

Memory researchers are beginning to believe that sleeping and dreaming, informal conversations, storytelling, and even passively watching mass media may be fundamental activities to the development, maintenance, editing, and retrieving of our long-term memories (Sylwester, 1995, p. 98). Because the development of long-term memory (learning) requires the physical reconstruction of the brain's neural networks, some neuroscientists believe it is necessary to shut down the neural activity during the building process. This may be accomplished during sleep or during daytime activities when the relevant neural network is not being used or is being used at a reduced level.

Primacy/Recency Effect
Average Primetime/Downtime

Learning episode length	Primetime	Downtime	Primetime	% Learning time
20 minutes	10 minutes	2 minutes	8 minutes	90
40 minutes	20 minutes	10 minutes	10 minutes	75
80 minutes	25 minutes	30 minutes	25 minutes	62

Figure 3.4

REHEARSAL AND RETENTION

The stability and permanency of the neural networks that constitute our ability to learn and remember are dependent largely upon the quality of the initial learning and the degree and quality of the practice or rehearsal that occurred during and after the learning episode (Sousa, 1998, p. 58). Rehearsal, or practice, is any processing of information that makes the information permanent and determines your ability to recall it (Wolfe, 1997). Rehearsals can be rote or elaborate. Rote rehearsal is the deliberate, continuous repetition of material in the same form in which it entered working memory. It takes time and effort and is not the most efficient way of remembering. Elaborate rehearsal requires integrating the material to give it sense and meaning. It organizes the information in a meaningful way. We use rote rehearsal to remember phone numbers or to memorize poems or dates, but we use elaborate rehearsal when we compare and contrast, explain similarities and differences, or critique and evaluate what we have learned. According to Sousa (1998), 80 percent of most rehearsal time is rote (p. 28).

Rote rehearsal is often necessary, and while it should be kept to a minimum there are some brain-compatible conditions that will make it more effective and efficient when it is used. According to Contine (1995), rote rehearsal is most effective immediately following the learning. It can be made more efficient by providing feedback to the student that is designed to reinforce correct trials and prevent practice errors from becoming embedded. Rote rehearsals should be based on a specific model, and practices should be kept to between five and fifteen minutes depending on the age of the learner (p. 55).

Some things should be taught by rote, but most things we teach in school students would learn more quickly and understand more deeply if we used elaborate rehearsal. Elaborate rehearsal involves higher-order thinking and problem-solving skills that engage the brain's frontal lobes. This engagement helps the learner make connections between prior knowledge, past experience, and the new learning. This in turn creates new neurological pathways and strengthens existing pathways, increasing the likelihood that the new learning will be consolidated and stored for future retrieval (Sousa, May, 1998, p. 27). When students move through the higher levels of Bloom's Taxonomy (or other thinking skills framework), they demonstrate a much greater depth of understanding of what they have learned.

IMPLICATIONS FOR THE BRAIN-FRIENDLY CLASSROOM

If we want students to master culturally important information and acquire skills they will need in the real world, as well as exhibit behaviors that will result in positive interpersonal relationships and intrapersonal fulfillment, students will need to have the opportunity to form and test their memories in simulated and real-life settings. Teachers will need to spend less time and energy on "covering the curriculum" and more time on using the knowledge that the students truly understand. The mission of the brain-friendly classroom should be, according to Sylwester (1995), "to help students begin to find relationships between the somewhat fact-filled experiences of school and to help them create and constantly test the memory networks that solidify those relationships" (p. 102).

When we are born, our brains have the potential to assimilate a large variety of stimuli. Over time we develop mental routines and patterns in response to the stimuli that are critical to our lives. Scientists call this process by which we develop selective mental patterns *neural pruning*. The brain-friendly classroom works to overcome neural pruning and to extend the neural networks. Current research indicates that significant brainwork can create more synaptic connections between the neurons, just as exercise can build muscle tissue. Our understanding and retention can be enhanced by creating classroom activities and experiences that meet our innate search for meaning and enhance the creation of memory and the efficiency of our ability to recall what we know.

Working to extend neural networks has important implications, according to Cardellichio and Field (March, 1998). It requires that students have opportunities to select and assimilate enough information so that they are forced to challenge misconceptions and to create strong, accurate conceptions. The first step in encouraging neural branching is to develop a structure or framework that will support the kind of inquiry that will improve the quality of the original learning and provide experiences that will allow the students to test and practice what they have learned in relevant and authentic ways. Three conditions appear to be necessary: relaxed alertness, active processing, and orchestrated immersion.

The low-threat/high-challenge classroom environment previously discussed characterizes relaxed alertness. There is nothing to suggest that the brain processes emotions and cognition separately. What we learn is inextricably a part of the total experience, including how we feel. In order for students to deal with complex ideas, pay attention, actively participate, and think either systematically or creatively, students must be rested, well fed, physically relaxed, and provided with opportunities to pursue their own interests (Caine and Caine, 1991). Relaxed alertness is not the same as being passive or calm. It is an openness and willingness to experiment and take chances, with positive anticipation or expectancy (Caine and Caine, 1991, p. 134). It is a function of the teacher's expertise and empathy and the degree of security and mutual respect found in the classroom environment.

Teachers can do many things to create this sense of relaxed alertness. Part of it is to demonstrate their own joy of learning and love of their subject matter. Another is to exhibit their artistry and ability in organizing the learning environment. Relaxed alertness exists in classrooms where the teacher introduces broad themes, where students work on projects that matter, and where positive social interactions between the teacher and the students and among the students themselves are encouraged. It is imperative to maintain an orderly and nurturing environment.

Some processing takes place automatically as we take in information and experience, but to gain deeper understanding and long-term retention we have to deliberately and consciously work for it. Active or meaningful processing is the consolidation and internalization of information by the learner in a way that is personally meaningful and conceptually coherent. Caine and Caine (1991, p. 46) suggest three means of causing students to actively or meaningfully process new information: reflection, contemplation, and creative elaboration. Each of the three increases the learners' responsibility for creating their own understanding of what has been learned and decreases the role that the teacher plays in guiding the students' cognitive process.

The students begin by checking and correcting their understanding with and without the assistance of teacher feedback (reflection). Next, they determine their personal meaning (contemplation), and then they reorganize the learning for application to new situations (creative elaboration). Specific classroom strategies to encourage the active processing of new learning include: student journals, the teaching of thinking skills, students becoming resident experts, panels and discussion groups, and projects and presentations involving community events.

Orchestrated immersion is defined by Caine and Caine (1991) as "taking information off the page and bringing it to life in the minds of the learners" (p. 46). The objective of the brain-friendly classroom should be to find ways to help students have experiences that are similar in complexity, challenge, and creativity to those they will experience in the real world. This can be accomplished most obviously through the creation of projects that are authentic and of personal interest to the student. It can also be accomplished by the use of multisensory representations of ideas or the use of stories, myths, and metaphors that assist the student in creating natural categories and provide positive emotional experiences.

There are also environmental factors that influence learning, such as the physical context of the classroom and the social relationships among the students and sense of community that exists within the classroom. These can be either inhibitors to the learning process or part of a complimentary climate that immerses the learner physically, emotionally, and intellectually into a carefully planned learning environment. Figure 3.5 compares the elements of orchestrated immersion as they might exist in the traditional classroom and in the brain-friendly classroom.

As teachers, our job is to invite and encourage students to experience and create. It is not a specific methodology. It is a grasp of what happens

Traditional Teaching vs. Brain-Compatible Teaching
Orchestrated Immersion

Elements of orchestration	Traditional teaching	Brain-compatible teaching
source of information	teacher to student	multiple sources
classroom organization	linear/individual	thematic/cooperative
classroom management	hierarchical	student responsibility
outcomes	specific/convergent	divergent

Figure 3.5 (Caine and Caine, p. 121)

in the brain during learning and selecting intelligently from among the methodologies at our disposal to orchestrate the students' experience in a way that is appropriate for the situation in which we find ourselves (Caine and Caine, p. 121).

SUMMARY

In this chapter we reviewed the way in which the brain processes information and determines what is selected for permanent storage, or learned. The workings of both short-term memory and long-term memory were discussed in terms of how neuroscientists believe they work and interact to create memories and alter neurological patterns that determine what we learn. Memories exist in many locations within the brain and differ in the ways in which they are formed and the ways in which they are recalled. Like attention, our emotions play a critical role in memory formation, as do meaning, past experience, and our understanding of future use and purpose. Teaching for meaning, memory, and understanding involves getting the students emotionally involved in the learning situation, helping students to determine the lesson's meaning for themselves, providing opportunities for the learners to meaningfully process what they are to learn, and focusing the learners on the major concepts and themes that define the task to be learned, remembered, and used.

REFERENCES

Caine, Renate and Geoffrey Caine. (1991). *Making Connections: Teaching and the Human Brain.* Alexandria, VA: Association for Supervision and Curriculum Development, 46–134.

———. (May, 1998). "Building a Bridge Between the Neurosciences and Education: Cautions and Possibilities." *NASSP Bulletin,* Reston, VA: National Association of Secondary School Principals. 82 (598), 1–8.

Cardellichio, Thomas and Wendy Field. (March, 1998). "Seven Strategies That Encourage Critical Thinking." *Educational Leadership,* Alexandria, VA: Association for Supervision and Curriculum Development. 54 (6), 33.

Contine, Tom. (1995). *Current Brain Research: Classroom Applications. "Brain Friendly Classrooms."* Kearney, NE: Educational Systems Associates, 16–55.

Cowley, Geoffrey and Anne Underwood. (June 15, 1998). "Memory." *Newsweek,* 49–54.

Goleman, Daniel. (1995). *Emotional Intelligence: Why It Can Matter More Than IQ.* New York: Bantam Books, 5.

Jensen, Eric. (1998). *Teaching with the Brain in Mind.* Alexandria, VA: Association for Supervision and Curriculum Development, 45–105.

Schacter, Daniel. (1996). *Searching for Memory.* Cambridge, MA: Harvard University Press.

Sousa, David. (1998). *Learning Manual for How the Brain Works.* Thousand Oaks, CA: Corwin Press, 28–58.

———. (January, 1998). "The Ramifications of Brain Research." *The School Administrator,* Alexandria, VA: American Association of School Administrators. 55 (1), 22–25.

Sylwester, Robert. (unpublished). "Memory—Acquiring/Editing/Recalling/Forgetting."

———. (1995). *A Celebration of Neurons: An Educators Guide to the Human Brain.* Alexandria, VA: Association for Supervision and Curriculum Development, 87–102.

Wolfe, Pat. (1997). "Translating Brain Research into Educational Practice." Seattle broadcast. Alexandria, VA: Association for Supervision and Curriculum Development.

CHAPTER 4

Brain-Compatible Instruction

The ability of teachers to employ appropriate strategies will be enhanced by an understanding of cognitive development and findings from brain research that ought to be a part of their ongoing education, especially as they strive to design lessons for individual learners.

Breaking Ranks

What we believe about the way that students learn has caused schools to traditionally emphasize rote learning, memorization of facts, and recall of information, with little emphasis on conceptual understanding and reasoning. These methods are proving woefully inappropriate for preparing future graduates, all of whom will need to be knowledgeable and flexible thinkers capable of understanding complex ideas. The traditional view of learning, focused as it is on knowledge and procedures of low cognitive challenge and superficial understanding, does not meet the demands of the present, nor will it serve students well in the future. What we thought we knew about how students learn shaped the decisions we made about what to teach and how to teach it. A fundamental tenet, therefore, in developing an instructional model for brain-compatible instruction must reflect what we are discovering about how students learn.

The brain learns because "that is what it does." According to Caine and Caine (1991), the brain has an inexhaustible capacity and, irrespective of age, sex, nationality, cultural background, or race, has a set of exceptional features:

- An ability to detect patterns and to make approximations
- A phenomenal capacity for various types of memory

- The ability to self-correct and learn from experience
- An inexhaustible capacity to create (p. 3)

Why then is learning such a struggle? "We have not grasped the way in which the brain learns," conclude Caine and Caine. "[W]e have assumed it learns by memorization of facts and skills" (p. 3).

There are aspects of classroom instruction that have been documented through theoretical research and empirical studies as leading to improved student learning. These ideas, popularized by Madeline Hunter and others, originate from the effective-teacher research conducted in the process-product and cognitive sciences. Most educators have come to believe that teaching is at least in part a science, with some practices and procedures that are demonstrably more effective than others (Germinario and Cram, 1998).

Efforts to establish a "model" for teaching, however, based on specific actions a teacher should take assumed that if the teacher performed the required elements, student achievement would increase. More recent conceptualizations of teaching and learning recognize that while this set of commonalties may exist, a teacher's decisions and actions are mediated by the teacher's mental models, the students' readiness and receptivity, the context of the instruction, and the climate of the classroom (Danielson, 1996). Brain-compatible learning involves acknowledging the brain's rules for meaningful learning and the organization of teaching with those rules in mind.

Several factors about how the brain works should shape the planning of instruction that is brain-compatible. Consideration must be given to the learners' needs:

- To understand the meaning of the material that is being presented
- To regulate to some degree their own learning and to actively construct meaning for themselves
- To collaborate with others in the process

As we become more familiar with the brain's capacity to seek and perceive patterns, create meanings, integrate sensory experience, and make connections, we will become better at organizing the content to be learned, the methods of delivering instruction, and the assessment of the learning process.

While having the learners construct meaning for themselves, actively participate in the lesson, and learn independently of the teacher may not appear to be new ideas, these attributes of brain-compatible teaching contrast sharply with the understandings upon which traditional instructional strategies are based. Learning, if it is to be a brain-compatible process, cannot be essentially a matter of responding to information as it is given. Since every complex event embeds information in the brain and links it to the rest of the learner's experience, past knowledge, and future behavior, the learner needs to be talking, listening, viewing, acting, and evaluating if learning is to take place. To meet this standard of brain compatibility, learning needs to encourage the learner to think about, understand, and apply the information to be learned in appropriate ways and in authentic situations both inside and outside the classroom environment.

Teachers preparing to provide this type of learning experience will need to have:

- A facility with a repertoire of instructional strategies that actively engage the learners, capturing their attention and sustaining the students' motivation to learn
- An understanding of how students learn
- A deep understanding of the learners' abilities, prior knowledge, and preferences for learning
- A general content knowledge and understanding of how their instructional content is related to it
- A specific knowledge in the content to be instructed and the materials and resources available to teach it
- Designated outcomes to be achieved by the students and assessments to measure those outcomes (Germinario and Cram, 1998)

What teachers and students will be doing in the brain-compatible classroom should be based on what we now know about teaching and learning. It should reflect a new paradigm of learning based on a constructivist approach to instruction and should cultivate a community of learners engaged in activities and decision making that will lead to the learning of important core content.

Much of what we believed to be good instruction is being validated through the direct observations of neuroscientists who can now see the electrical and chemical response of the brain as it learns. However, experts in brain-compatible learning claim that much of traditional instruction is at odds with how the brain learns, and that the typical classroom environment actually inhibits the brain from learning.

HOW BRAIN RESEARCH IS INFLUENCING PRACTICE

Brain-compatible instruction is not a packaged program. It is an acknowledgement that when teachers have a thorough understanding of how the brain develops, learns, and organizes itself, they will make better decisions about instruction (Sousa, December, 1998). Research on learning is quickly catching up with our curiosity about the human brain. Until very recently most of what we thought we knew about brain functioning was derived from the visible and somewhat measurable manifestations of cognition rather than from the direct observation of the cognitive mechanisms and processes we are rapidly learning so much more about. Teaching and learning have been separate acts related only through correlation and supposition that certain teacher actions increased the probability that learning would take place (Germinario and Cram, 1998). To the classroom teacher, learning was and is a covert act. But the recent research provides us with a more complete understanding of brain functioning, and the educational implications for instruction are more frequently being discussed by researchers and practitioners alike.

American thought on the process of learning, according to Gerald Bracey (1994), has been influenced alternately throughout our history by British Empiricists such as Locke and Hume, Continental Rationalists such as Descartes and Leibnitz, and early psychologists such as Thorndike, Skinner, and Piaget. But it was Piaget who laid the foundation for the most promising understanding of human learning through research that led him to conclude that the growth of knowledge was the result of individual constructions made by the learner (Brooks and

Brooks, 1993). Piaget was the first to suggest that cognition was fueled by the learner's attempt to make sense of what is going on.

As we have seen in the earlier chapters, the human brain uses sensory/perceptual processes to take in information, experiences, events, and objects from the environment. It then draws on related memories, problem-solving skills, and automated responses to determine the importance of the stimulus and to eventually respond.

In addition to our gaining the understanding that learning is an active and constructive process, it has also became abundantly clear that learning is more powerful when it is done in concert with others as part of a group. Deborah Miere (1992) succinctly states the conventional wisdom inherent in this finding when she writes,

> Human beings are by nature social, interactive learners. We check out our ideas, argue with authors, bounce issues back and forth, and ask friends to read our early drafts, talk together after seeing a movie, pass on books, attend meetings and argue our ideas, share stories and gossip to extend our understanding of others and ourselves. Talk lies at the heart of our lives (p. 3).

Learning, therefore, not only is situated in the physical environment of the classroom and dependent upon what the teacher and an individual student may do, but occurs in a social context that can be more powerful and effective when conducted as a group.

To learn something, a student must actively relate it to other knowledge, either in a way that makes sense to the student based on what he already knows or in a way that modifies his current understanding so that the new information can be accommodated. This is a reflective process that takes time and one that can be strengthened by the student's interaction with others. In order for an instructional strategy to be brain-compatible, it must provide meaning for the learner, actively engage the learner in the learning activity, and provide a learning environment that is collaborative.

The implications of brain research for classroom practice cut against the grain of some traditional school practices although they are in line with some current reform efforts. As Sylwester writes, "The cognitive sciences are discovering all sorts of things that good teachers have always done.

What's important, however, is that our profession is now getting support for many practices that critics have decried" (1995, p. 139).

Understanding how our brain develops, the role of our emotions, and how our brain processes information provides insight into how we can best deliver instruction, organize curriculum, and orchestrate the learning environment. In general this implies both subtle and dramatic changes in how the classroom and the school should be organized. For example, we now know that the brain has critical periods at which it demands certain types of input in order to create and consolidate its neural networks. What a child learns during these so-called "windows of opportunity" strongly influences what may be learned after the window closes (Sousa, December, 1998). By understanding the different times and areas of brain growth, we can better decide how best to approach content and skills in the curriculum and how to provide a brain-friendly classroom environment.

By knowing how to capture a student's attention and how retention can be enhanced, we are better prepared to organize instruction and integrate the curriculum in ways that will improve learning. Knowing that how students feel about a learning situation determines the attention they will devote to it highlights the importance of a physically safe and emotionally secure classroom and increases the importance of teaching students about their emotions and how to better manage them. Recognizing that the brain makes new neural connections when it is actively engaged in interesting and challenging activities emphasizes the need for busy and interactive environments that are multisensory, task centered, and socially interactive.

Brain-compatible teaching takes a holistic and systematic approach to instruction that helps the teacher organize the available alternatives to traditional teaching techniques. The old teacher-in-charge, factory model of lecture, memorization, and assessment characterizes traditional teaching by regurgitation. While many teachers provide variation on this basic model with innovative teaching techniques and methods of assessment, most still hold to the common characteristic of the teacher directing the learning. Brain-compatible instruction is a collaborative process where students and teachers share responsibility for the pedagogical dynamic in ways that challenge our mental models of teaching and learning.

As we have seen (chapter 1), we all have mental models of the teacher's role and the process of learning. These are deeply held assumptions that are physiologically entrenched as a result of our early experiences in school (Caine and Caine, May, 1998, p. 7). Consequently, traditional instruction is focused on the memorization of surface knowledge, is dominated by the teacher, and is based on traditional resources such as textbooks, lectures, and visuals. Traditional assessment is based on quantitative data and is measured with multiple-choice or true/false tests designed to find out whether students can answer the teacher's or the textbook's questions. And discipline in the traditional classroom is defined as maintaining those good behaviors that enable the students to absorb information that the official curriculum or teacher lesson plan determines.

The brain-compatible classroom, as described by Caine and Caine (May, 1998), has the following attributes:

- An emphasis on meaningful learning versus memorization
- The establishment of meaning and the patterning of information to be learned
- The integration of the curriculum through the use of complex themes and stories that establish relevance
- A recognition of the brain's capacity as a parallel processor and its ability to perform many functions simultaneously
- Lesson segments and schedules tied to the time it takes to learn a skill
- Alternate assignments
- Alternate ways to assess student achievement
- Students' responsibility for their own behavior and group progress (pp. 45–46)

Achieving the contrasting mental models that underlie these very different approaches to instruction and learning (figure 4.1) cannot happen through direct teacher training or by teaching specific skills, but, it is possible to form new mental models through the use of brain-compatible teaching and learning strategies and by practicing it with the entire school. Brain-compatible learning must become the dominant model, and such a shift cannot be imposed or brought about in a mech-

Traditional Classroom Based on Outmoded Models of Learning	Brian-Compatible Classroom Based on Current Brain Research
part-to-whole presentation of material, with emphasis on discrete skills and facts	whole-to-part presentation of material, with emphasis on concepts and processes
students viewed as empty, passive vessels	students viewed as interactive participants and thinkers
teacher disseminates information	teacher facilitates learning
focus is on single correct answer	focus is on points of view and problem-solving skills
assessment is separate	assessment is ongoing and integrated with learning
student works alone or with the teacher	students work alone, in pairs in small and large groups, and with the teacher and other adults

Figure 4.1 Contrasting Mental Models

anistic or fragmented way. As is indicated in chapter 8, it will be brought about when the three conditions of relaxed alertness, orchestrated immersion, and continuous active processing exist for the entire school community.

Instructional delivery is brain-compatible when students are encouraged to become active rather than passive participants in the lesson. It is less brain-compatible when the classroom teacher consistently uses only one or a limited number of delivery models, to the neglect and exclusion of others (Contine, 1995).

KEY ELEMENTS OF BRAIN-COMPATIBLE INSTRUCTION

To achieve brain-compatible instruction, careful consideration must be given to how the material is organized, how it is presented to the students, and what the students are expected to do with it. Careful consideration must also be given to the classroom climate, both physical and psychological, and the assessment of learning must be an integral part of the lesson design.

Sensory Engagement

Brain research confirms that we learn best when we are actively involved in interesting and challenging situations and when we interact with others during the learning process. This can best be accomplished through the consistent use of instructional strategies that are multisensory, in classrooms that are visually appealing, and through classroom activities that cause the students to stand up, move about, and discuss with one another what they are learning while they are learning. Teachers need to have access to technology and other resources that will make the classroom an engaging and interesting place. They need to be encouraged to make their classrooms visually appealing places where teachers and students both learn and teach. This type of social engagement is emotionally stimulating and enhances the learning process (Sousa, January, 1998).

Attention

We educators must use the basic mechanisms and processes that regulate attention if we are going to make valid application of what we are learning from brain research. Brain-compatible instruction must take into account that our attention systems are designed to quickly recognize and respond to change. In schools students must be prepared to attend to subtle and gradual changes. To assist learners in doing this, teachers must identify and focus on what is important, sustain student attention by eliminating irrelevant stimuli, and help students access memories that could be relevant. Teachers should adapt their instruction to these built-in biases and should strive to use imaginative teaching and management strategies that enhance their students' ability to pay attention (Calvin, 1996).

Meaning

Meaning has a great impact on whether information and skills will be learned and stored, and what we already know acts as a filter to help us determine what it is that is meaningful to us. To convince a learner to persist with an objective, the teacher must help the student establish meaning. There are several ways in which students can be aided in their quest for meaning. Teachers can begin with answering "why" questions, by pointing out patterns, by teaching taxonomies for grouping information, and by teaching patterns of cause and effect, compare and contrast, and similar relationships that establish connections between what is to be learned and what the learner may already know. If we expect students to find meaning, the curriculum must contain connections to their past experience, and relevant connections must be made between and among subjects. Integrating the curriculum increases meaning and retention, especially when students recognize a future use for what it is they are learning (Jensen, 1998).

Retention

We now know that discrete facts, vocabulary, and concepts can only be learned and retained with the expenditure of an inordinate amount of neural energy, practice, and time. Disconnected information can only find its way into the brain's permanent memory through repetitive, rote practice and will seldom be transferred to new or novel situations. Our task should be to help students begin to find relationships in the fact-filled experience of school and help them create and constantly test the memory networks that solidify those relationships. Retention and recall are enhanced by the quality of the original learning experience, the emotional importance that the learner attaches to that experience, and the opportunity to practice the new learning. When classroom experience consists of authentic thematic classroom learning, the amount of retention is doubled (Jensen, 1998).

Classroom Environment

Learning can be facilitated or inhibited by the conditions within the classroom. The human brain has a finite supply of energy, and whenever this energy is diverted from learning tasks in order to relieve stress, threats, anxieties, or embarrassments, the probability of learning is decreased. Brain-compatible classrooms are well organized, appropriately decorated places where students feel good about themselves. When classes are fragmented, physically uncomfortable and cliquish students are left feeling less competent, uncomfortable, and rejected, which impedes the learning process. Under these conditions students may suffer anxiety in the classroom. They worry about how to please the teacher, about whether they will ever understand what is being taught, and about how their classmates will react to their mistakes (Harmin, 1994).

DESIGNING BRAIN-COMPATIBLE LESSONS

Designing lessons that are brain-compatible requires selecting those teacher behaviors, student behaviors, and classroom management techniques that make the most sense in terms of what we think we now know about brain functioning and organizing those activities into a model for instruction and a classroom environment that will facilitate the learning process.

The initial steps in designing a lesson that will enhance the student's ability to learn involve capturing the student's attention. Recognizing how our attentional systems work, we should begin a brain-compatible lesson with a creative lesson introduction that captures the student's attention and focuses the student on the highlights of the learning to take place. A brain-compatible lesson must:

- Set the stage for the learning and focus the students' attention
- Shape the students' attitude about the lesson
- Build bridges between new information and what the students will learn
- Direct student attention to relevant information
- Assist the teacher in selecting the appropriate instructional behaviors (Contine, 1995)

It is important to focus the students in the initial stages of the learning and to have them tuned in at the beginning of the lesson, gaining early access to their memory systems. Students come to class with a variety of experiences and knowledge, and the beginning of the lesson should help the students access the relevant experiences and knowledge to which the new learning can be linked. In designing a brain-compatible lesson introduction, three things should be considered:

- How can I focus the learners with something of personal interest, involving prior experience, or so novel as to capture their attention?
- How can I associate and organize the information to be learned so that the material will be meaningful, relevant, or useful in ways that will hold the students' attention?
- How can I actively involve the learners in cognitive and physical activities that will result in learning?

At the beginning of a lesson, the students' minds can be anywhere—they could be thinking about another class, something that happened outside of school, something that happened at home, or something they need to do or plan to do later that day. Gaining their attention can be done in many ways. Carol Cummings (1990) suggests several subject areas that can capture their attention:

- Anything that relates to the students personally
- A discrepant event, something the students are not expecting
- Emotionally involving the students through the teacher's enthusiasm
- Humor or drama
- Raising concern by telling the students what is expected of them

Other important aspects of a brain-compatible lesson are the lesson objectives and teacher expectations. What the students are expected to learn and be able to do must be at a level of difficulty that is neither too easy (thereby failing to sustain the students' attention) nor so difficult that the students' level of frustration would cause them to be unable to remain focused. Students need, as was previously discussed, to feel safe and challenged. To attain this state of relaxed alertness as part of the lesson design it is important to specify objectives and teacher expectations early in the lesson. Students should be provided with information about the nature of the task at hand and helped to understand precisely what is expected of them. When lesson objectives and teacher expectations are shared:

- Students know generally and specifically what is to be learned
- Guesswork is taken out of the learning process
- Students gain a sense of direction and security
- Students are given a framework for evaluating personal achievement and success

Since learning is the process of linking new information to what we already know, we can maximize the learning of new material, according to Cummings (1990), by:

- Providing lesson overviews
- Outlining information using headings or graphic organizers
- Listing objectives
- Having students predict learning outcomes

Teacher behaviors and the organization and presentation of the learning material can also enhance or inhibit the learning process. In order to capitalize on the brain's natural process and to assist students in learning and retaining information, brain-compatible lessons must consider several issues. Lessons that emphasize relevance and use diverse motivating strategies to arouse interest increase the probability that the learner will remain focused. When the teacher presents materials and provides the input of the lesson, the students' mental process is assisted if the teacher provides visuals, concrete examples, models, and hands-on involvement. Time also needs to be deliberately provided for the students to mentally organize and structure the new information for themselves and to rehearse their responses to questions the teacher might pose. These are physical responses that may be required as part of the learning activity.

Brain-compatible lessons have two critical attributes. First, they are clear about what it is the student is to learn. Second, they engage both the teacher and the students in specific learning behaviors that will lead to accomplishing the objective. Each of the teacher's actions, explanations, questions, directions, activities, assignments, and responses to student questions and behaviors should be made with the process of cognition in mind.

We know that the brain needs time to process information and time to engage in collaboration with other learners if the new learning is to be understood and retained. This information processing must be observable and carefully monitored by the teacher. The brain-compatible lesson must provide time for both covert and overt active participation on the part of the learner. *Covert* participation is the individual's mental processing of what is to be learned. *Overt* participation is the product or physical performance produced by the student that indicates that learning has taken place.

Teachers, if they are to be effective in developing the deeper and more complex understanding of content necessary to genuine learning, must take advantage of the methods that depend less on the teacher and more on what students can learn by working both independently and together. Student-centered approaches suggested by our current understanding of how we learn are proving to be most effective. Research suggests that strategies that involve students directly in their own learning provide for both deeper understanding and longer retention. Specific strategies include:

- Seminars
- Cooperative learning activities
- Debates and dialogues
- Field experiences
- Independent studies
- Laboratory experiments

A teacher-dominated classroom, yn which the teacher is the purveyor of knowledge, punctuating her or his dissemination of information with only occasional questions, leaves students unengaged. While lecturing will always have its place and may remain as an appropriate method for some maturial, students who are exposed to only teacher-centered instruction are left with a narrow and superficial understanding of the content presented.

The teacher as facilitator, utilizing a wider range of learning activities, can better guide the learning process for students with varying learning styles. While some may argue that good teachers have always included in their teaching the facilitation of learning through student activities, John Goodlad (1984) found in his studies a "low incidence of activities involving active modes of learning" in 1983, and little has changed.

To create the kind of reflection, active engagement, and collaboration envisioned by a constructivist approach to learning, pedagogy must orient itself towards higher-order thinking skills, such as drawing inferences, making judgments, engaging in logical reasoning, and solving problems. This transition can most easily be accomplished by embedding problems in the existing curriculum. Perhaps the best example of how that has been done can be found in the "Habits of Mind" model used by the Central Park East Secondary School in New York City. Students are deliberately taught to:

- Weigh evidence
- Consider varying points of view
- See connections and relationships
- Speculate on possibilities
- Assess value both for society and for themselves

Robert Sylwester, in *A Celebration of Neurons: An Educator's Guide to the Human Brain* (1995), describes the classroom of the future as one that will

focus more on drawing out existing abilities than on precisely measuring one's success with imposed skills, encourage personal construction of categories rather than impose existing categorical systems, and emphasize the individual personal solutions of an environmental challenge over the efficient group manipulation of the symbols that might represent the solution (p. 23).

Research on the brain overwhelmingly supports this type of personal engagement of the learner. When compared with traditional classrooms, the ones in which students are actively engaged in the learning process through interaction with the teacher and with each other show gains in the following areas (Cummings, 1990):

- Academic motivation to learn
- Understanding and retention
- Attitudes toward peers
- Self-esteem and ethical behavior
- Cooperation and problem-solving skills

Elements of Student Engagement

- Presenting content in a way that connects new information to what a student may already know.
- Creating activities that cause the student to interact with the content by solving problems that are relevant or authentic to the student.
- Grouping students in different patterns to provide and enhance engagement opportunities.
- Pacing lessons to allow for thinking, construction of meaning, and closure on the part of the student.
- Providing feedback to students on how they are progressing as part of the instructional experience.

Figure 4.2

Students need to master these areas to succeed in the next century.

If we accept Danielson's (1996) pronouncement that "engaging students in learning is the raison d'être of education," then the brain-compatible classroom must be built on instructional strategies that immerse students in the process of learning and the active construction of their personal understanding of what it is they are expected to learn. Elements of this type of student engagement are listed in figure 4.2.

Several instructional strategies—some new, some old, and many revisited—can be used by teachers to create the community of learners that appears to be at the heart of creating brain-compatible classrooms in which all students meet the more rigorous demands that the future holds for them. At the core of many of these strategies is a cooperative classroom in which students can be grouped in many ways for instruction. They include students working individually, in large groups led by the teacher or a student, small groups working independently or with the teacher's guidance, homogeneous groups, heterogeneous groups, partners, triads, and other configurations conducive to the activity or consistent with the learner's preference.

Encouraging, acknowledging, and rewarding the student's efforts are also important ingredients in designing a brain-compatible lesson. Feed-

Effective and Ineffective Uses of Praise

Praise is effective when it is . . .	Praise is ineffective when it is . . .
consistent	random or unsystematic
specific	global
spontaneous	bland
for attainment	for participation
noncomparative	comparative
for effort and ability	for ability only
after the process is completed	distracting to an ongoing process

Figure 4.3

back in general and positive reinforcement of the learners' efforts helps the students maintain their focus and keeps them engaged in the learning activity. The students feelings about themselves and the lesson will determine how much effort they will put into the class. Students must see the connection between their effort and the result. They need immediate and specific feedback on whether their work is right or wrong to sustain their attention.

Praise and acknowledgement, even when it is given verbally, may actually enhance a student's attention (Cameron and Pierce, 1994). According to Brophy (1981), it is most effective or least effective when it is used as described in figure 4.3.

A lesson summary enables the brain to analyze, synthesize, and internalize the information presented. Brain-compatible lessons must provide time and activities that allow the brain to organize the essence of the lesson, make sense of it, and tie the key points of the lesson into a coherent whole. According to Cummings (1990), several variables under the teacher's control enhance or inhibit the process of retention and recall. They include the quality of the original learning (the models, the examples, and the establishment of meaning during the learning activities) and the meaningful processing and practice of the information, skills, or behaviors to be learned.

Brain-compatible lessons must incorporate multisensory inputs. Verbal activities such as reading, listening, and writing, all of which involve

Criteria for Brain-Compatible Lesson Design

- Instructional goals should be clear and stated in terms of student learning instead of student activity.
- Instructional goals should be capable of assessment and appropriate to the diverse students in a teacher's charge.
- Instructional goals should be translated into learning experiences that should progress from easy to hard, from simple to complex, and from attention to one domain of learning to integration across several.
- Time allocations should be reasonable, with opportunities for students to engage in reflection and closure.

Figure 4.4

symbol manipulation (the weakest capability of our brain), must be balanced with nonverbal kinds of experiences involving visual activities and tactile–kinesthetic experiences. Lessons must also be designed to assist the learner in making associations and creating patterns from unorganized material.

An effective lesson must also provide opportunities for students to be active in the learning, to construct their own meaning, and to process what has been taught. As Shuell (1986) writes: "Without taking away from the important role played by the teacher, it is helpful to remember that what the student does is actually more important in determining what is learned than what the teacher does" (p. 423).

According to Cummings (1990, p. 107), "Information is likely to remain inert if it is not processed," and information will remain inert even if it is relevant to new situations. Strategies that invite students to process information include opportunities to develop questions; give a summary; relate the learning to their own experience; predict an outcome; compose a metaphor, analogy, or visual representation of what they have learned; and evaluate the importance of what has been learned.

The processing of information itself can be more or less effective depending upon the amount of processing time, when the processing takes place and for how long, and the nature of the processing activity.

Generally speaking, the processing of information should begin with the integrated whole and then go on to an analysis of the parts. Short periods of processing time should be provided on a frequent basis during the initial learning, and recall and practice opportunities should be provided intermittently over an extended period of time. Last but not least, the processing opportunities should provide the students with a variety of applications of the new learning.

Brain-compatible lesson design emphasizes the importance of the students' taking responsibility for their own learning (see figure 4.4). It provides a rationale for moving away from instructional methods created to address what are fast becoming outmoded conceptualizations of how students learn, such as methods and classrooms in which:

- Teacher talk dominates the lesson
- Teachers rely heavily on textbook structure and resources
- Students are discouraged from collaborating
- Activities are focused on low-level cognitive skills and convergent thinking
- Learning is measured using traditional assessment techniques

To embrace brain-compatible teaching, educators must begin to make an important paradigmatic shift described as "abandoning the mimetic approach to learning and implementing practices that encourage students to think, demonstrate and exhibit" (Brooks and Brooks, 1993, p. 116).

Merrill Harmin, in her book *Inspiring Active Learning: A Handbook for Teachers* (1994), describes the need for lessons that are organized so that class periods proceed smoothly, are interesting, and have high student involvement. To accomplish this Harmin suggests lessons that:

- Are fast paced enough to keep all students actively involved
- Return to topics from time to time rather than aiming for mastery at any one time so that learnings are reinforced over time and the risk of losing student involvement is minimized
- Provide sufficient variety in the classroom to keep students involved yet not so diverse as to threaten student security and need for predictability

SELECTING BRAIN-COMPATIBLE STRATEGIES

Lessons that include both questioning and discussion of subject matter become valuable as a brain-compatible strategy only when they elicit student reflection and challenge deeper student engagement. But forming cooperative or collaborative groups is only a beginning in creating the kind of intellectual involvement required for brain-compatible instruction. In addition to the now-popular cooperative learning strategies and activities in use in many classrooms, teachers will need to think deliberately about the nature of the activities and interactions that comprise these cooperative endeavors.

A teacher's skill in questioning, leading discussions, and fostering collaboration among students is critical to providing both individual and group interactions that truly engage the student or students in the process of learning. The *Socratic Seminar* is an effective strategy that provokes student thinking and dialogue and is a unique alternative to the traditional class discussion, because students do almost all of the talking. In a Socratic seminar, students are seated in a circle and are prompted by an open-ended question that encourages them to engage one another in a thoughtful dialogue. Unlike the traditional question and answer, in which the teacher poses rapid-fire, short-answer, and low-level questions to individual students, the Socratic Seminar focuses on carefully crafted questions that enable students to reflect on their understanding. Students are allowed time to think, students are expected to explain the thinking behind their responses, and other students are encouraged to elaborate on the responses given.

Discussions are animated by important questions in which all students are engaged. When run well:

- The teacher does not hold center stage
- Students are encouraged to comment on one another's responses
- Thinking is illuminated and initial responses are probed and expanded

Transforming a classroom from a traditional format to a brain-compatible one can begin as simply as altering:

- The physical setup of our classroom—from rows of seats to a circle or circles
- The way in which we pose our questions—from single response to open ended
- The time we wait for a student's response—from 2–3 seconds to 8–12 seconds
- The ways in which we accept those responses—from teacher affirmation to affirmation from peers

Other brain-compatible approaches to learning include strategies adapted from *information processing models* such as those developed by Hilda Taba, Bruce Joyce, and William Gordon (Canady and Rettig, 1996). A sampling of those techniques are summarized in figure 4.5.

Equally effective are time-proven methods such as simulations and learning centers. *Simulations* are best described as reality. They serve as active classroom experiences in which participants are provided with lifelike problem-solving activities. When constructed well and implemented effectively, they provide a variety of experiences to extend and deepen the students' understanding of the substance upon which the simulation is based.

Learning centers too can be effective brain-compatible activities, providing individual students, pairs of students, or small groups of students the opportunity to:

- Practice skills learned in a larger group
- Extend skills or knowledge beyond those acquired in the large group
- Rehearse for an assessment
- Practice or remediate skills not mastered earlier

Technology can also provide a significant vehicle for creating a more individualized and interactive learning environment and can assist teachers in creating communities of learners. Teachers need to consider the many ways in which technology can be incorporated into their classrooms and consider the use of not only the computer but videodisc technology and CD-ROM and the Internet. These technological tools can make the investigation of more complex tasks feasible by providing stu-

Summary of Information Processing Models
Applicable to Brain-Compatible Instruction

Concept Development	Designed to guide students through the process of categorizing information and synthesizing information in order to make generalizations.
Concept Attainment	Requires students to develop a definition of a selected concept through the examination of critical attributes and nonexamples.
Synetics	The use of analogies and metaphors to encourage creative thought.
Memory Models	Association techniques to link new information to that which is familiar.

Figure 4.5

dents with the opportunity to work at higher levels of cognition. Technology can also shift the control for learning from the teacher to the student by providing for a wide range of learning styles and meeting individual needs.

A necessary outgrowth of raising student expectations and altering instructional strategies to meet that challenge will be the reconsideration of the ways in which student achievement will be assessed. As instructional goals become increasingly complex and as methods of classroom instruction become more diverse, so must our approaches to assessment. A minimum requirement for any brain-compatible instructional strategy must be that it can be assessed in a meaningful way. A well-designed approach must include the specific ways in which student work will be evaluated; and to the extent possible, the student should know up front the required standards against which his project or performance will be measured. To be most effective, assessment methods should reflect authentic and real-world application of the skills and an understanding of the content being assessed. But the full power of assessment in the brain-compatible classroom is the way it provides feedback to students on what they have learned and reflection to the teachers on what they have taught. Meaningful assessment provides information to both the student and the teacher as they plan the next steps in the learning process.

A BRAIN-COMPATIBLE CLASSROOM CLIMATE

An outgrowth of providing brain-compatible interactive learning experiences is the concept of building a community of learners. If the teacher is no longer the single source of knowledge, then students and the teacher begin to interact in different ways in the learning process, both teaching and learning. The attitude of the teacher and the relationships between students and teacher both affect the outcome of the lesson. The classroom must have a climate of low threat and high challenge, a climate of relaxed alertness. Students do not try as hard if the teacher doesn't care. Research indicates that when students experience a caring teacher, they evidence "academic, social, and ethical benefits, including greater enjoyment of the class, stronger motivation, and stronger feelings of social competence" (*Breaking Ranks: Changing an American Institution,* 1996, p. 96). Caring affects the receptivity of the students to teaching and the acquisition of knowledge.

The importance of emotions to learning makes teaching a matter of relationships — relationships that should be grounded in a mutual respect between the students and the teachers. Teachers can cultivate this mutual respect by their interactions with the students and the type of interactions they encourage among the students they teach. A classroom conducive to learning is one in which students and the teacher engage in activities of value and in such a way as to encourage students to take risks in a safe environment. Charlotte Danielson (1996) describes a "culture for learning" when she writes that classrooms should be "cognitively busy places with students and teachers setting high value on quality work" (p. 96).

Many students suffer anxiety in the classroom, which is inimical to the learning process. While some tension may need to exist in the classroom, too much tension can cause students to "downshift" and resist engagement in a learning activity. Some students worry about what the

Truth Signs

We each learn in our own ways.
It's okay to make mistakes.
It's intelligent to ask for help.
Everyone needs time to think and learn.
We learn more when we are willing to risk.

Figure 4.6

teacher thinks of them, whether they will understand what is being taught, and how their classmates will react to the mistakes they may make. Teachers who want to create brain-compatible classrooms will need to have strategies for dealing with those anxieties.

G. H. Pilon (1991) suggests two simple techniques for creating a comfortable and respectful classroom. One suggestion is to post "truth signs" around the room to remind students of important truths about learning and life. The signs do not tell students what to do but remind the students of important ideas related to the learning process. Examples of truth signs are listed in figure 4.6.

Posted truth signs alone do not guarantee that students will not feel anxious. A steady offering of support is also usually necessary. To reinforce the truth signs, Pilon suggests a strategy called cushioning, which involves raising student awareness of how the truths are related to learning by inviting students to apply these truths to learning. This can be done by asking students questions at the beginning of a lesson, such as "Is it okay to make mistakes?" and allowing students to discuss briefly how making mistakes shows we are trying, taking risks, and how we learn from the mistakes we make.

In *Inspiring Active Learning: A Handbook for Teachers* (1994) Merrill Harmin lists several factors that infl uence a student's willingness to participate and gives direction for providing a caring learning environment. They include:

- Providing opportunities for students to succeed
- Making students feel important
- Reducing student anxicty
- Providing students with choices
- Pacing instruction for the student comfort
- Providing both teacher and student-to-student support

A brain-compatible classroom is comfortable, respectful, and businesslike. It is a classroom in which noninstructional routines and procedures are well established, where the teacher and the students have a mutual respect, and where they are engaged in activities that support the stated instructional purposes of the learning.

SUMMARY

Current brain research and the implications drawn from it suggest a new paradigm of teaching and learning that may prove critical as we plan for instruction for the 21st century. Brain-compatible classrooms will need to be communities of learners in which students are actively and cognitively engaged in the learning process in ways that are collaborative and allow students to construct their own understanding.

Through this brain-compatible approach to learning it is believed that the students' understanding will be deeper and more complex, that the knowledge they acquire will be retained longer, and that the probability of their transferring that knowledge to real-world situations in new and creative ways will be enhanced.

The brain-friendly classroom will need to be a caring and interactive environment. Teachers will need to rethink both their instructional strategies and their classroom management to accommodate a wide variety of teaching methods and to encourage respect and rapport, both among the students and between the students and themselves. Much of what they need to do can be accomplished by modifying traditional methods and by increasing their knowledge of what is constantly being discovered about how we learn.

REFERENCES

Bracey, Gerald. (1994). *Transforming Americas Schools: An Rx for Getting Past Blame*. Arlington, VA: American Association of School Administrators.

Breaking Ranks: Changing an American Institution. (1996). Alexandria, VA: National Association of Secondary School Principals.

Brooks, J. G. and M. G. Brooks. (1993). *In Search of Understanding: The Case for Constructivist Classrooms*. Alexandria, VA: Association for Supervision and Curriculum Development.

Brophy, J. and J. Alteman. (1991). "Activities as Instructional Tools: A framework for Analysis and Evaluation." *Educational Researcher,* 20 (4), 9–23.

Caine, Renate Nuemmella and Geoffrey Caine. (1991). *Making Connections: Teaching and the Human Brain*. Alexandria, VA: Association for Supervision and Curriculum Development.

———. (May, 1998). "Building a Bridge Between the Neurosciences and Education: Cautions and Possibilities." *NASSP Bulletin*. Reston, VA: National Association of Secondary School Principals. 82 (598), 1–8.

Cameron, J. and W. Pierce. (1994). "Reinforcement, Reward, and Intrinsic Motivation: A Meta-Analysis." *Review of Educational Research,* 64 (3), 363–423.

Canady, Robert L. and Michael R. Rettig. (1996). *Teaching in the Block Strategies for Engaging Active Learners*. Princeton, NJ: Eye on Education.

Contine, Tom. (1995). *Current Brain Research: Classroom Applications. "Brain-friendly" Classrooms*. Kearny, NE: Educational Systems Associates.

Cummings, Carol. (1990). *Managing a Cooperative Classroom: A Practical Guide for Teachers*. Edmonds, WA: Teaching Incorporated.

Danielson, Charlotte. (1996). *Enhancing Professional Practice: A Framework for Teaching*. Alexandria, VA: Association for Supervision and Curriculum Development.

Germinario, Vito and Henry Cram. (1998). *Change for Public Education Practical Approaches for the 21st Century*. Lancaster, PA: Technomics Publishing.

Goodlad, John L. (1984). *A Place Called School*. New York: McGraw-Hill.

Harmin, Merrill. (1994). *Inspiring Active Learning: A Handbook for Teachers*. Alexandria, VA: Association for Supervision and Curriculum Development.

Jensen, Eric. (1998). *Teaching with the Brain in Mind*. Alexandria VA: Association for Supervision and Curriculum Development.

Miere, Deborah. (Summer, 1992). "Reinventing Teaching." *Teachers' College Record*. New York: Teachers' College Press.

Pilon, G. H. (1991). *Workshop Way*. New Orleans, LA: Workshop Way Incorporated.

Shuell, T. (1986). "Cognitive Conceptions of Learning." *Review of Educational Research*, 56, 411–436.

Sousa, David. (January, 1998). "The Ramifications of Brain Research." *The School Administrator*, Alexandria, VA: American Association of School Administrators. 1 (55), 22–25.

———. (December, 1998). "Is the Fuss about Brain Research Justified?" *Education Week*, 35, 52.

Sylwester, Robert. (1995). *A Celebration of Neurons: An Educator's Guide to the Human Brain*. Alexandria, VA: Association for Supervision and Curriculum Development.

"Understanding the Brain—Educators Seek to Apply Brain Research." (September, 1995). *Education Update Newsletter*, Alexandria, VA: Association for the Development of Supervision and Curriculum. 37 (7), 1, 4–5.

CHAPTER 5

Brain-Based Curriculum

Despite ongoing reform efforts, the nature of classroom practice, the processes and content of instruction in public school classrooms of today are little different from what they were in 1980 or 1970.

M. Smith and J. O'Day

The curriculum of a school is generally considered the formal and informal content and process by which learners gain knowledge, develop skills, and alter attitudes, beliefs, and values. The curriculum, whether planned, unplanned, inferred, or hidden, is both sponsored and legislated by the school. In short, it is the stuff around which schooldays are structured and learning is, eventually, measured (Cushman, 1991).

Throughout the twentieth century three distinct orientations to curriculum theory have been the focus as to what and how students should learn.

Intellectual traditionalists have held that the substance of the curriculum should be derived from what we have always expected students to know, which is built around a background in the classics and a cultural literacy that comprises a common core of knowledge. Traditionalists argue that the student's interests and interests of the society are best served when all students are steeped in tradition (usually Western tradition) and given a common access to the "best" ideas that the human race has achieved. Educators subscribing to this framework tend to view students as recipients of knowledge and support the organization of that knowledge into separate and discrete disciplines and units of study.

Social behaviorists believe in a more scientifically determined curriculum. Focusing on the behaviors of successful people, they suggest the use of that information forms the basis for what students will need to know and be able to do. Their approach to curriculum views the student as a resource to be altered, and the substance of what might be taught has been heavily influenced by the politics and economics of the community that the school serves. In contrast to the intellectual traditionalists, whose common core knowledge spans the boundaries of culture, literacy, history, place, and individual preference, the social behaviorists are more deeply concerned with the techniques of curriculum delivery.

Experientialists suggest that any curriculum should start with the interests and concerns of the learners. Ultimately, based on those naturally occurring interests, teachers should construct projects and activities to help the students understand the problems that comprise the common human experience. Learners are viewed as partners in the school experience. Emphasis is placed on process, and the curriculum tends to be without a traditional organization or definition (Shubert, 1993). Simply stated, this curricular orientation arises from the adage that we learn from our experience. A growth metaphor, rather than a product or process metaphor, best characterizes the experientialist's focus.

The most important issue in curriculum development is deciding what learning content and learning experiences will most benefit students in the future. Decisions as to the nature of what students should know will drive expected learning outcomes and standards. These decisions are eventually translated into a coherent curriculum that is not simply a collection of disparate pieces but provides a sense of unity, connectedness, relevance, and authenticity.

Within this context, Germinario and Cram (1998) provide a set of principles to guide twenty-first century curriculum development. These include:

Success for all learners. While teachers often speak to reaching all students, a disparity exists between the ideal and what actually happens (Lortre, 1975). Curriculum for the twenty-first century must emphasize learning outcomes, where each student demonstrates competencies before moving on.

Appropriate content. Discussions regarding the development of a core set of knowledge that students should learn at a given grade level have become the centerpiece of educational reform in many states. Using a modified Delphi approach, Uchida, Cetron, and McKenzie (1996) obtained consensus from a panel of over fifty leaders in education, business, and government. From their responses a list of major academic content areas students needed to master for success in the twenty-first century was developed. This list included:

1. Math, logic, and reasoning skills; functional and operational literacy; and an understanding of statistics.
2. Critical interpersonal skills, including speaking, listening, and the ability to be part of a team.
3. Effective information-accessing and -processing skills using technology.
4. Writing skills to enable students to communicate effectively.
5. Knowledge of American history and government to function in a democratic society and an understanding of issues surrounding patriotism.
6. Scientific knowledge base, including applied science.
7. An understanding of the history of the world and of world affairs.
8. Multicultural understanding, including insights into diversity and the need for an international perspective.
9. Knowledge of foreign languages.
10. Knowledge of world geography.

Integration and authenticity. Relevant links among and between learning objectives are critical to the curriculum of the twenty-first century. When such a curriculum is in place, young people are more likely to integrate educational experiences into their schemes of meaning, which in turn broadens and deepens their understanding of themselves and their world (Beane, 1995).

Social and cultural responsibilities. Curriculum must prepare students to understand their society and its multiplicities of cultures. A school that is truly committed to teaching about diversity reinforces the curriculum with ongoing interdisciplinary opportunities for students to learn about culture, develop cultural sensitivity, examine their own biases (and the biases of others), and develop skills necessary to communicate effectively with all types of people and to survive in a multicultural world. Specific objectives common to multicultural programs include:

- Knowing about and feeling proud of one's own culture and ethnic identity
- Knowing about and appreciating cultures different than one's own
- Recognizing contributions that all types of people—women and men, young and old, rich and poor, including those from minority and atypical cultures—have made to the school, community, nation, and world
- Developing skills for communicating effectively with people from different backgrounds
- Recognizing and refusing to accept any behavior based on stereotypes, prejudice, or discrimination
- Recognizing the economic interdependence among nations

Critical thinking and reasoning. Schools of the twenty-first century must promote increasing opportunities for students to take greater responsibilities for their learning. Students are confronted with information at an astounding rate. Increasingly, students must be prepared to identify, analyze, manipulate, and draw conclusions about what they see, hear, and read.

Technology. Technology is one way to provide significant tools for teachers and students to develop an information-rich instructional environment to solve problems more efficiently, enhance thinking operations, organize and process information, communicate ideas, learn new information, reinforce prior learning, and apply learning to future life situations.

The research on student learning clearly reflects the importance of technology in today's schools. Specifically, the effective use of technology can be linked to improved problem-solving skills, increased student motivation, and higher levels of academic achievement. It is extremely important that today's schools have the capability of delivering instruction in a climate that is conducive to learning and can facilitate technology as a learning tool.

Computers and other technology are fast becoming a frequent sight in America's classrooms. Unfortunately, all too often they are used as electronic workbooks or seen as a separate type of content. Curriculum for the twenty-first century must infuse technology into the content of every learning unit. The interactive, high-performance uses of technology could allow students to solve real-world problems, retrieve information from electronic libraries, perform scientific simulations and experiments, travel to far away places, and analyze large volumes of information.

Standards and accountability. What gets measured, gets done (Peters, 1987, p. 480). Systematic data collection of student outcomes must become part of the curriculum for the twenty-first century. The primary principle of this activity, however, must be to improve student learning. This process should be consistent with current knowledge about how learning takes place and provide continuous feedback for the student.

Methods of assessment must be linked to authentic learning objectives and include methods such as observations, interviews, projects, tests, experiments, portfolios, and journals.

While the concepts just stated provide a conceptual framework for thinking about curriculum, they do not address the emerging body of knowledge that links cognitive science and brain research. Using current learning theory, curriculum would be focused around the creation of events and the introduction of materials and ideas that encourage the development of neural network connections in students. When this occurs, the curriculum becomes *constructivist,* that is, one where students construct individual meaning from the processing of information and activities.

A CONSTRUCTIVIST-ORIENTED CURRICULUM

Constructivism is based on the premise that by reflecting on our experiences, we construct our own understanding of the world we live in.

Through this reflection, each of us generates our own mental models, which are used to make sense of our experiences. Learning, therefore, becomes the process of adjusting mental models to respond to new experiences.

Brooks and Brooks (1993) provide guiding principles that help operationalize constructivism as a learning theory. These principles include:

- Learning is a search for meaning. Therefore, learning must start with the issues around which students are actively trying to construct meaning.
- Meaning requires understanding wholes as well as parts. Parts must be understood in the context of wholes. Therefore, the learning process focuses on primary concepts, not isolated facts.
- In order to teach well, we must understand the mental models that students use to understand the world and the assumptions that support those models.
- The purpose of learning is to construct one's own meaning, not to have the "right" answers by repeating someone else's meaning. Learning is inherently interdisciplinary, and the only valuable assessment of learning is assessment that is part of the learning process and that provides students with information on the quality of their learning.

The use of constructivism in the design of curriculum would lead to the elimination of standardized curriculum. Curricula would then become customized to the prior experiences of students by using raw data, primary resources, and activities that relate to real-world problems.

These authors provide a comparison of the constructivist-oriented curricula and that which is traditionally utilized in schools (p. 17).

Traditional Classrooms	**Constructivist Classrooms**
Curriculum is presented part to whole, with emphasis on basic skills.	Curriculum is presented whole to part, with emphasis on big concepts.
Strict adherence to fixed curriculum is highly valued.	Pursuit of student questions is highly valued.

Curricular activities rely heavily on textbooks and workbooks.	Curricular activities rely heavily on primary sources of data and manipulative materials.
Students are viewed as blank slates onto which information is etched by the teacher.	Students are viewed as thinkers with emerging theories about the world.
Teachers generally behave in a didactic manner, disseminating information to students.	Teachers generally behave in an interactive manner, mediating the environment for students.
Teachers seek the correct answer to validate student learning.	Teachers seek the students' points of view in order to understand students' present conceptions for use in subsequent lessons.
Assessment of student learning is viewed as separate from teaching and occurs almost entirely through testing.	Assessment of student learning is interwoven with teaching and occurs through teacher observations of students at work and through student exhibitions and portfolios.
Students work primarily alone.	Students work primarily in groups.

TOWARD A COHERENT CURRICULUM

In most schools there is a mismatch between the emerging learning theory based on the cognitive sciences and the dominant educational curriculum and practices. In short, the human mind is much better equipped to gather information by interacting with it rather than reading about it, hearing lectures on it rather than studying abstract models.

It is estimated that we essentially learn and retain approximately:

- 10 percent of what we hear
- 15 percent of what we see
- 20 percent of what we both see and hear
- 40 percent of what we discuss
- 80 percent of what we experience directly or practice doing
- 90 percent of what we attempt to teach others

Yet, despite this representation, schools seem quite satisfied building curricula around words, symbolic representations, and abstractions. Often, curricula are written that emphasize the acquisition of information generated from a textbook. Largely, the presentation is teacher-directed, from a premise that all students learn in essentially the same way (i.e., telling students about something is the primary method to convey knowledge).

Caine and Caine (1991) conclude that the biggest mistake schools make is the fragmentation of content. They go on to say that "teaching bits and pieces has been the focus of teaching; further, the brain is looking for meaningful connections; [teachers] actually cut those off" (p. 1).

To address this pervasive practice, curricula must be written (and instruction delivered) that enhance the learner's natural tendency to seek patterns and make meaning of the learning situation with which they are confronted. Curricula then must be written so that the pieces of information hold together and make sense as a whole. Beane (1995) characterizes this phenomenon as a *coherent curriculum*. He describes the notion of *coherence* as beginning with the view of the curriculum as a broadly conceived concept that is about something. It is not simply a collection of disparate parts or pieces that accumulate in student experiences and on transcripts. "A coherent curriculum has a sense of the forest as well as the trees, a sense of unity and connectedness, of relevance and pertinence. Parts or pieces are connected or integrated in ways that are visible and explicit. There is a sense of a larger, compelling purpose, and actions are tied to that purpose" (p. 3).

He further describes the salient features of coherence in curriculum, which include:

- Creating and maintaining visible connections between purposes and everyday learning experiences
- Creating contexts that organize and connect learning experiences
- Enhancing the sense of purpose and meaning for the learner
- Exploring how the learner makes sense out of the experience

Beane concludes that

the search for coherence does not mean simply clarifying purposes in the existing curriculum. Rather, it suggests that creating coherence involves

connecting parts or pieces of the curriculum, identifying meaningful contexts for information and skills, and helping young people and adults
make sense of learning experiences (p. 4).

The importance of coherence extends beyond a commonsense perspective. There is significant evidence from the neurosciences that
speak to the brain's laterality. That is, there are significant differences
between the left and right hemispheres of the brain. Yet, in a healthy person, the two hemispheres dynamically interact. Caine and Caine (1994)
thus conclude that "the two-brain doctrine is most valuable as a
metaphor that helps educators acknowledge two separate but simultaneous tendencies in the brain for organizing information. One is to
reduce information into parts; the other is to perceive and work with it
as a whole or series of wholes" (p. 91).

CHARACTERISTICS OF A BRAIN-COMPATIBLE CURRICULUM

Throughout this book, brain-compatible strategies have been
addressed to deal with most every aspect of school life. Those same
concepts and strategies should be utilized in the development and writing of curriculum. Margulies (1991) provides a summary of the con
cepts that should be embodied in a brain-compatible curriculum.
These include:

- *Absence of Threat*—Content and learning opportunities are
  both challenging and achievable; additionally, the curriculum must promote a trusting relationship between the
  teacher and the student.
- *Meaningful Content*—The content of the curriculum must capitalize on the learner's innate search for meaning; consideration should
  be given as to whether the content is from real life, relates to students' prior knowledge, is developmentally appropriate and thus
  understandable, and can be learned within the life of the learner. In
  short, the curriculum should encourage the search for meaning with
  mental models such as patterning and mapping.

- *Choices*—In a brain-based learning environment, students should have multiple opportunities to discover and process information based on their preferred learning styles. There should be inquiries and projects that address a variety of critical thinking levels and the students' multiple intelligences. Choice activities should facilitate students' understanding of key concepts and can also be used as authentic assessment tools. Students can be guided to make activity choices that are challenging for them. Providing choice opportunities promotes active processing and helps build student self-esteem.

- *Adequate Time*—The limitless amount of information that exists and that learners are confronted by has provided what Wurman (1989) calls "information anxiety." He describes it as the widening gap between what we understand and what we should understand. To address this phenomenon, curriculum must be structured so that students can reflect on the content, contemplate, and get feedback from others. In doing so the student learns not only about the subject, but also how it relates to his/her own life.

- *Enriched Environment*—Caine and Caine (1994) emphasize the need to take information off the blackboard and bring it to life in the minds of the students. Thus, the need exists for curricula containing opportunities for learning through multisensory, complex, real projects. Neuroscience suggests that enriched environments increase dendritic branching, fostering better communication between nerve cells. Jensen (1998) concludes that an enriched environment that is consistent with brain-based learning provides frequent challenge, continual novelty, and dramatic feedback.

- *Collaboration*—Curricula must provide opportunities for students to work together toward a common goal. Activities must be provided for students to acquire and practice communication and social skills. Working together on common learning tasks fosters a sense of learning community and encourages meaningful discussion and reflection. Cooperative learning opportunities are typically appropriate vehicles to integrate into the curriculum, since they involve the interaction of cognitive and social goals through the solving of common learning problems.

- *Immediate Feedback*—Feedback provides a pathway for both attention and emotion. Our brain thrives on feedback for growth in learning and reinforcement of (or change to) mental models and provides information needed to survive. Feedback produces a surge from neurotransmitters that invokes a dynamic emotional response. To provide necessary feedback, curricula must change to include real-world experiences. Kovalik (1994) describes the real world as having a great deal of built-in feedback for learners. Such first-hand feedback is instantaneous and more intrinsic (and thus more powerful) than feedback from an outside source, the teacher, or the answer sheet for the workbook or reading kit (p. 101).
- *Mastery*—Creating meaningful curriculum dictates that authentic assessment be conducted to determine what and how students have learned. These assessments must be ongoing, since in brain-based learning all learning is a process and related to the ongoing lives of the learners. Jensen (1998, pp. 282–283) describes several ways that the human brain can evidence learning. They include:

1. **As data or information:** The learner can replay the data back to the teacher, but it rarely has meaning—the learner still needs to sort it out and make relevant connections. . . .[U]ntil the learner does sort it out, it's meaningless to him/her.
2. **As meaning:** Information is transformed by the learner. . . .[H]ere the learner discovers, for him/herself, the patterns, the relationships, the themes, useful tie-ins or the interdisciplinary connections.
3. **As a new or better working model:** . . . A system . . .a conscious or nonconscious set of organizing principles of how something works ("democracy is run by special interest groups" or "democracy works best when . . .").
4. **Specific, useful "how-to" strategies and skills:** . . .These are usually embedded as procedural memories and are often called "body learning." . . .[E]xamples would be playing an instrument, building a model, hitting a baseball, working a microscope, etc.
5. **Attitudes:** . . . Perceptual bias and opinions have changed; these open or close the "gates" of learning. . . .[H]ow you feel about a topic or subject is quite critical. . . .[D]o you feel positive about the topic, like it or want to learn more?

6. **Observable behavior changes:** . . .Many neuroscientists would say that unless there is a corresponding change in physical behavior, we cannot say that biologically, something has been learned. In other words, cognition or auditory descriptions of content understanding is not integrated until the whole body is involved in learning.

7. **Internal:** . . .How this learning affects you personally and also implications for your past, present and future. The more connections you make, the greater the neural mapping.

While the foregoing concepts provide a useful conceptual framework to guide curriculum development, the key elements of a brain-based curriculum center on the teacher providing a vehicle for students to see patterns among the content presented and to use what they learned in relevant problem-solving situations.

Kovalik (1994) provides criteria for determining the brain compatibility of a written curriculum:

- It is *locally based* and invites the teacher to select a physical location, easily visible, upon which to base instruction.
- It *provides a rationale*—a why—for teaching the content and explains what one hopes to accomplish by teaching it.
- It *clarifies* what it isn't and what it does not intend.
- *Content is stated as concepts*—giant patterns from which significant key points can be easily derived and molded to best fit a teacher's particular group of students and their prior knowledge. Because the statements are conceptual in nature rather than factoid, and thus rich in pattern-detecting potential, pattern-seeking is built in naturally and easily for both teachers and students.
- *One is not left to one's own devices* to come up with what is important to know, yet there is real flexibility in making the best possible fit with specific students, their prior experience, knowledge, interests, etc.
- *A picture of "so what?"* is provided. What would it look like if students learned this well and were able to use what they had learned?
- *Hooks for integrating* other content areas are built in—California history with science as well as math and language (pp. 122–123).

THE INTEGRATIVE CURRICULUM

Clearly, cognitive science research has provided a framework for how we can maximize student learning potential. Concepts related to memory, emotions, the impact of threat, patterning, and the brain's constant search for meaning all dictate that curriculum must be integrated across disciplines and learning opportunities.

Current research on both learning and curriculum design clearly establishes that teaching subjects in isolation distorts knowledge. A curriculum that is discipline-based makes learning artificially fragmented, and there is reason to be concerned that the fragments may never cohere. While disciplines can help to organize our thinking, they should not be the focus of instruction. Disciplines are an efficient vehicle for coverage but not for learning. Sylwester (1996) reinforces this concept by stating,

> Unfortunately, our culture seems to value random facts, and schools tend to reinforce this bias . . .Our task as educators, however, is to help students begin to find relationships between the somewhat random, often trivial fact-filled experiences of everyday life and the fewer enduring principles that define life—and then to help them create and constantly test the memory networks that solidify those relationships (p. 102).

We have known for a long time that students learn more, remember more, and apply knowledge more when they are taught in an interdisciplinary mode. Students need to see the whole context of what they are learning (Wells, 1992). Drawing connections between subjects requires students to do more higher-level thinking, making for a richer learning experience. Retention is increased because information that has multiple connections is simply better remembered.

An interdisciplinary approach can also help to bring order to the chaotic curriculum being created by the knowledge explosion. It can lend coherence to the abundance of content by showing how the substance of what students may be expected to learn is interrelated.

Defining the *integrative curriculum* is not a simple task. Yet it tends to have several common elements that distinguish it from the traditional subject-based curriculum. Shoemaker (1989) characterizes those elements in providing the following definition: Integrative curriculum "cuts across subject-matter lines, bringing together various aspects of the curriculum into meaningful association to focus upon broad areas of study." It reflects the interdependent, real world, and involves the learner's body, thoughts, feelings, senses, and intuition in learning experiences that unify knowledge and provide a greater understanding than that which could be obtained by examining the parts separately.

The integrative curriculum bases its practices on the characteristics of the human learner and on the interdependent nature of reality. Instead of artificially dividing the world into "subjects" and using text-books and seat work, integrative education immerses students in an enriched environment that reflects the complexities of life. This pro-vides a holistic context for learning that leads to a greater ability to make and remember connections and to solve problems (Kovalik and Olsen, 1998).

No universal model for implementing an integrative curriculum exists. Moreover, the thematic approach with the associated changes in both teaching and assessment require much greater effort to create qual-ity integrative curriculum. Ross and Olsen (1993), acknowledging the complexity involved in moving from subject discipline-based to inte-grative forms of curriculum define five models that provide a sequence for implementation that builds on itself.

First, there is "single-subject integration," which presents the content of one curriculum subject as it appears in real life and requires students to apply skills within this meaningful context.

Second, in the "coordinated model," two or more teachers teach inte-grated single subjects to the same students separately but cooperatively, to ensure that the desired skills and content are taught.

Third, in the "integrated core model," one teacher remains with stu-dents for two or three periods. For example, a teacher might teach lan-guage arts in the context of science or social studies as the "core" around which the rest of the school day is planned.

Fourth, in the "integrated double core model," two teachers instruct the same students within two integrated cores. For example, one might teach math skills in the context of science, while another teaches lan-guage skills within a social studies context.

Finally, in the "self-contained core model," one teacher with multiple-subject credentials remains with one group of students all day, teaching all skills and content.

The most common method of operationalizing an integrated curriculum is through *thematic instruction*. Thematic instruction is the organization of curriculum around global themes that integrate basic disciplines such as reading, math, and social studies. The theme, then, provides the basis for exploration of broad topics and/or solving problems related to the theme. This type of instruction assists the brain in the creation of patterns, or neural pathways, that are connected in larger patterns of related information. This pattern-seeking mechanism in the brain is facilitated through the use of thematic teaching in that it provides a big picture for the brain to perceive.

Fogarty and Stoehr (1995) conclude that the use of a global theme to cover overlapping skills and concepts from various content is both appropriate for and inviting to student learning. The big ideas overarching different content provide obvious, visible, and known connections from one subject area to another. These ideas become recursive in the learning and create strong neural pathways.

In short, the theme serves as a cognitive structure that facilitates pattern identification and recognition of the interrelationships among concepts, places, events, and timeframes. Kovalik (1994) describes several important functions of the theme:

- For students, it is a powerful tool, enhancing their capacity to more effectively process, store, and retrieve what is learned; to anticipate what comes next; and to generalize to other students
- For the teacher, it serves as an organizer for curriculum building and material gathering throughout the year, providing a thread that connects one month to the next, as well as relating everything to organized concepts for the entire year
- For both teacher and students, it establishes the game plan for the day, month, week and year (p. 140).

The development of a thematic, integrated curriculum begins when teachers (and at times students) *choose a theme*. The themes almost always involve a large integrated system, such as the town in which students live, and broad concepts, such as political governance systems, weather, and demographics. Typically, the theme is relevant to the everyday lives of the students.

The next step is for teachers to *design the curriculum,* organizing and integrating the various subject disciplines around the theme. Consideration must be given to learning objectives that facilitate both content knowledge and process skills.

As the curriculum writing is completed, *instruction must be designed* that moves learning into an integrated context so the brain can identify like patterns and link ideas to one another. Thus, it is imperative that a brain-compatible teaching-learning perspective be within the discipline and applied beyond the discipline with connections to real-life events.

Fogarty (1997) suggests that instructional strategies that best facilitate brain compatibility within a context of thematic instruction are problem-based learning, projects and case studies.

Finally, the nature of the instructional activities encourage *presentation and celebration.* Since thematic instruction is often problem solving or project oriented, it frequently involves students' giving collective presentations to their class, school, or community. Sylwester (1995) describes the significance of emotional events and memory by stating,

> Because the limbic system plays important roles in processing both emotion and memory, emotion is an important ingredient in many memories. Memories formed during a specific emotional state tend to be easily recalled during events that provoke similar emotional states. Classroom simulations and role-playing activities enhance learning because they tie curricular memories to the kinds of real-life emotional contexts in which they will later be used (p. 44).

A recent Educational Research Service publication (ERS, 1999) cites the potential benefits of curriculum integration and thematic teaching, which include:

• *Emphasis on relevance and meaning.* The encouragement of students to think about real-life issues provides a basis for the brain's innate search for meaning and connections. This, in turn, promotes higher-order thinking and long-term understanding.

- *Student engagement and active learning.* Students can take a more active role in directing their own learning by solving problems and developing theories and questions related to the theme.
- *Opportunities to meet the needs of diverse learners.* Slower learners can focus on essential information within a context of relevance and meaning. Advanced learners can extend their study beyond what they may already know.
- *Teacher professional growth.* Teachers have more opportunities for collaboration, including the sharing of ideas and resources.
- *Parent involvement.* Parents can share and contribute their expertise in the development of curriculum. Community members can participate by becoming a resource for field trips and as speakers in the classroom.

BRAIN-BASED INTEGRATED CURRICULUM—WHAT IT LOOKS LIKE

A review of the literature indicates that curriculum integration that leads to relevance, meaning, and, ultimately, neural connections can occur in many different ways. Models exist along a continuum regarding the scope and involvement of the integration. Yet, to be truly successful, the curriculum must conscientiously incorporate the brain-based learning concepts and strategies embodied throughout this book. By doing so, the benefits associated with providing for the brain's innate need for meaning will be conducted in an enriched environment that is free from threat; this immerses the learner in relevant content and provides for the active processing of the knowledge and skills that have been learned.

When a productive school culture has been developed and the school community is ready to integrate a curriculum, the first (and arguably the most important) step is to select a theme for student study. Barab and Landa (1997) have developed conceptual parameters that effectively guide the selection of a theme. The theme:

- Applies broadly or pervasively across disciplines
- Is legitimate for the disciplines in which it will be used

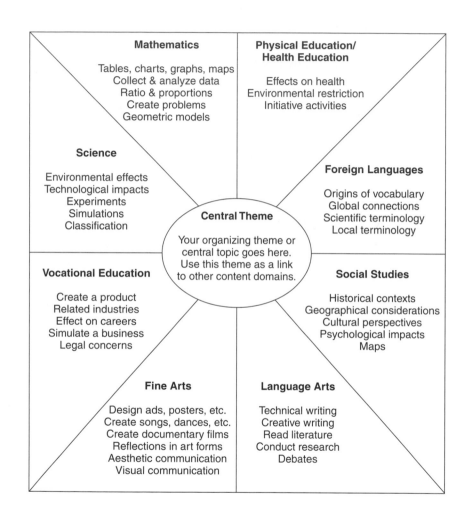

Figure 5.1 Curricular Connections Planning Wheel.
Modified from the work of Joan M. Palmer (Maute, 1992).

- Reveals similarities and differences
- Is perceived as important by the learners
- Is likely to connect to students' experiences
- Promotes creative and critical thinking
- Applies to the real world
- Is complex enough to accommodate a wide range of activities
- Is age-appropriate
- Accommodates learners of diverse cultural backgrounds and learning styles

Once a theme is chosen, teachers (and, when appropriate, students, parents, and other community members) generate a variety of topics and activities related to the theme. Maute (1992) has developed a rubric that demonstrates how cross-curricular connections can be made by following a "Curricular Connections Planning Wheel" (see figure 5.1). While this Planning Wheel is very useful as a framework to guide integration, other concepts such as technology, interpersonal and cooperative skills, specific higher-order thinking skills, and media and research skills can easily be added to the model.

Figure 5.2 provides an integrated curriculum related to the introduction of world languages and cultures to elementary school students. Specifically, a rationale for study is provided, then it outlines objectives and activities related to specific district-wide proficiencies standards, and, finally, assessment strategies guide unit and daily planning. This particular unit integrates proficiencies and activities within geography, language arts, economics, human relations, social studies, history, and music.

Figure 5.3 provides an example of an integrated curriculum where students decided upon the theme. In this case, the district was in the process of planning for the construction of a new school. Students chose the theme, since they would eventually be attending the school. Figure 5.3 describes the curriculum content standards that are addressed. Figures 5.4, 5.5, and 5.6 are sample lessons associated with the unit; figure 5.7 provides additional lesson options and culminating activities.

Rationale

Children who learn a second language should do so while learning the culture and customs of a land for which the language is the native tongue. Increasing knowledge of another country and people and making connections to what is known about one's own culture is likely to improve retention and enjoyment of foreign languages. In this program, children will be learning words appropriate to the concepts in the native language of the country they are studying.

Course Description

Proficiency

	I. Introduction to Culture and Language
Geography	A. What we know/want to know
Economics	*Objective:* Students will be introduced to a country through artifacts displayed around the room.
	1. Discuss what we know/want to know, and chart
	2. Make suitcase (construction paper) to hold souvenirs
Geography	B. *Objective:* Students will locate country on world map.
	1. Make flag of country/locate on map
	2. Provide world map worksheet, and color country
Economics	C. *Objective:* Students will examine artifacts from country and draw conclusions about culture.
	1. Culture box — put together box of artifacts — eating/kitchen items, household items; writing/reading school supplies; play items
	2. Teacher models looking at item; what it's made of — guess its use
	3. Students will do the same in small groups
	4. Groups share objects and conclusions with whole class

What did you learn about the culture of _____(country)_____?

Social	D. Introduce language
Science	*Objective:* Students will learn words of friendship and courtesy in the language of the country and

(*continued*)

through the remainder of the course of study
and use them throughout the day.

1. Extend through games for numbers, color
   names, days of week

II. Literature

Language Arts/Human Relations

A. *Objective:* Student will be immersed in country's literature by being read to and reading with the teacher everyday fiction and non-fiction materials.

B. *Objective:* Student will use Venn diagrams and other activities to compare/contrast similar stories from United States and the country.

C. *Objective:* Students will be provided opportunities for dramatic presentations of favorite folktales or stories.

III. Natural History

Geography

A. *Objective:* Students will become aware of the common plants and animals of the country through use of assorted resources.

B. *Objective:* Students will become aware of the physical features of the country through use of assorted resources. Students may use what they know in creating maps of the country.

C. *Objective:* Students will become aware of the weather of the country through use of assorted resources, including the Internet. Students will keep a weather chart for daily weather and compare to Moorestown's weather. Students will discuss impact of weather on people's choices for clothing and shelter.

IV. Shelter

Social Science/ Economics

A. *Objective:* Students will become aware of shelters used in the country and how they vary according to the type of community (rural, urban). Students will design a model of a shelter typical of the country.

(continued)

Social Science/ Economics	V. Food A. *Objective*: Students will become aware of the main foods of the country through use of assorted resources B. *Objective*: Students will refer to a world map to locate the country. Have students brainstorm why the main foods are prevalent. Students will make food following simple recipes from their country.
Human Relations/ Social Science	VI. Clothing A. *Objective:* Students will become aware of the traditional dress of the country and compare to clothing worn on a daily basis. B. *Objective:* Students will create dolls in traditional dress and learn the language for clothing items.
Human Relations/ Social Science	VII. Games and Toys A. *Objective:* Students will learn the rules, language and instruments and toys needed to play the games of these countries. B. *Objective:* Students will be able to make games and teach the games to small cooperative groups. Games and toys will be related to games American children play.
Human Relations/ Social Science	VIII. School Life A. *Objective:* Students will become aware of the education system of the country. B. *Objective:* Students will compare their school experience to schooling in the country.
Human Relations/ Economics	IX. Customs A. *Objective:* Students will learn about the distinct cultural practices of the country and act out classroom vignettes of everyday life.
History	X. Holidays and Celebrations A. *Objective:* Students will become aware of the many festivals and holidays throughout the year.

(*continued*)

XI. Arts

Fine Arts/
Social
Science

A. *Objective:* Students will be introduced and have opportunities to participate in traditional music and dance that highlight the culture of the country. Students will be able to sing and dance to songs that may correspond to holiday celebrations in these countries.

B. *Objective:* Students will be able to produce art work, relics and artifacts that reflect the people, places and language symbols of the country.

World Language
Music Activities

Suggested Songs/Dances/Instrumental

Peru
Vidalita
Arre, Borriquito
My Farm
Arre, Caballito
A Tall Tale

Kenya
Gogo
Yoo, Yoo
Mokong 'ondi
Kaiyeu nanu
Wakarathe
Abot tangewuo
Oh Ketejo nongusia
Nyingunyan denyo
Tekele lomeria
Chemworor
Sukuru ito

Japan
Japanese Rain Song
Sakura
This Road or That
Momotaro—Japanese Legend
The Moon
The Rabbit
Wild Bird

France
Sur le Pont d' Avignon
Are You Sleeping? (Frere Jacques)

(continued)

Hold Tight (Tenes las de Pres)
I've Been to Gather Mussels (A la Peche des Moules)
The Goat (La Chevre)
Tete Epaules
Fais Dodo
A Wise Old Owl
Never in Our Mountains
Dansons la Capucine
Chibreli (French Folk Dance)
Mon Papa
The Carillon (Le Carrillon)
Three Drummer Boys
A Little Ship
A Rat and the Cat (Un Rat et le Chat)

Strategies to Consider When Assessing and Evaluating Students

A-1 • Criterion referenced tests
A-2 • Research projects
A-3 • Observations of and interviews with students
A-4 • Essays
A-5 • Portfolios
A-6 • Experiments
A-7 • Student surveys designed to measure interest in learning science
A-8 • Community projects
A-9 • Self-evaluations
A-10 • Class discussions
A-11 • Problem-solving exercises
A-12 • Decision-making activities
A-13 • Reflective logs and journals
A-14 • Demonstrations and exhibitions of student work
A-15 • Laboratory activities

Figure 5.2 *Integrated World Language Curriculum. (Reprinted with the permission of the Moorestown Township Public Schools, Moorestown, New Jersey.)*

Cross-Content Workplace Readiness Standards

All students will use technology, information and other tools.

All students will use critical thinking, decision-making, and problem-solving skills.

All students will demonstrate self-management skills.

Visual Arts

All students will acquire knowledge and skills that increase aesthetic awareness in dance, music, theater, and visual arts.

All students will refine perceptual, intellectual, physical, and technical skills through creative dance, music, theater, and/or visual arts.

All students will utilize art elements and arts media to produce artistic products and performances.

All students will demonstrate knowledge of the process of critique.

All students will develop design skills for planning the form and function of space, structures, objects, sound, and events.

Language Arts Literacy

All students will speak for a variety of real purposes and audiences.

All students will listen actively in a variety of situations to information from a variety of sources.

All students will write in clear, concise, organized language that varies in content and form for different audiences and purposes.

All students will read various materials and texts with comprehension and critical analysis.

All students will view, understand, and use non-textual visual information.

Mathematics

All students will develop the ability to pose and solve problems in mathematics, other disciplines, and everyday experiences.

All students will communicate mathematically through written, oral, symbolic, and visual forms of expression.

All students will connect mathematics to other learning by understanding the interrelationships of mathematical ideas and the role of mathematics.

All students will develop spatial sense and an ability to use geometric properties and relationships to solve problems in mathematics and in everyday life.

All students will develop, understand, and use measurement to describe and analyze phenomena.

All students will develop an understanding of patterns, relationships, and functions and will use them to represent and explain real-world phenomena.

Science

All students will gain an understanding of the structure, dynamics, and geophysical systems of the earth.

All students will develop an understanding of the environment as a system of interdependent components affected by human activity and natural phenomena.

Social Studies

All students will learn democratic citizenship and how to participate in the constitutional system of government in the United States.

All students will learn democratic citizenship through the humanities, by studying literature, art, history and philosophy, and related fields.

All students will acquire historical understanding of political and diplomatic ideas, forces, and institutions throughout the history of New Jersey, the United States, and the world.

All students will acquire historical understanding of economic forces, ideas, and institutions throughout the history of New Jersey, the United States, and the world.

All students will acquire geographical understanding by studying the world in spatial terms.

All students will acquire geographical understanding by studying the environment and society.

Figure 5.3 Curriculum Content Standards Addressed by This Unit. (Reprinted with the permission of the Moorestown Township Public Schools, Moorestown, New Jersey.)

Objective: Students will examine the problem associated with student overcrowding in a school building.

Activity Description:
1. Students will analyze the current and projected student enrollments for the school district.
2. Students will list possible reasons for the increase in student population.
3. Students will answer the question: Are the increases greater at the elementary, middle, or high school grades?
4. Students will examine the legal occupancy limits of the five schools.
5. Students will discuss the question: What can we do to make room for additional students in the middle school?

Materials:
    District Enrollment Data (copy for each student)
    Chart Paper (for teacher to list any relevant points for lesson 2)
    Lined Paper (for students)
    Pencils
    Markers

Figure 5.4 Sample Lesson

Objective: Students will gain an understanding of architectural terms and materials used when a building is being constructed.

Activity Description:
1. Students will brainstorm ideas answering the question: "What do you need to build a building?"
2. Student and/or teacher will create a master list on chart paper.
3. Students will be introduced to the following vocabulary:
   a. land and title
   b. survey
   c. utilities: sewer, water, electricity
   d. bid, cost of labor; cost of materials
   e. architect
   f. contractor
   g. blueprints
4. After discussing definitions, the students will put the vocabulary words and definitions into journal response booklets.
5. Students will create a bid for a small project; example: dog house, doll house.

Materials:
   Journal Response Booklets (composition book or a book the shape of a house)
   Chart Paper
   Pencils
   Markers

Figure 5.5 *Sample Lesson*

Objective: Students will develop a list of materials needed in a classroom that will meet the educational needs of students and teachers now and in the future.

Activity Description:
1. Students brainstorm ideas to answer the question: "What does a classroom need to meet the needs of students and teachers over the next 30 years?"
2. Student and/or teacher create a master list on chart paper.
3. Students will meet in small groups to discuss which symbols should be used to represent each item.
4. Students gather together and share information. A list of the symbols is created and put on chart paper.
5. Students will put symbols in journal response booklets to be used when making blueprints of a classroom.

Materials:
Journal Response Booklets
Pencils
Chart Paper
Markers

Figure 5.6 Sample Lesson

- Review changes in the blueprints, from one stage to another
- Examine the cost of materials in the construction process
- Investigate the role, function, and impact of lighting, acoustics, and climate on the construction process
- Research and study various architectural elements
- Tour the building site and meet the architect(s)

Culminating Activities

- Two speakers: the architect and superintendent
- Build a scale model of the school, from plan to elevation (3–4 weeks)
- Serve as ambassadors to incoming students and members of the community by conducting tours of the building (2 weeks)

Figure 5.7 *Additional Lesson Options*

Regardless of the theme chosen or the subject areas addressed, it is important that the framework be built around brain-friendly concepts and instructional activities. From a practical standpoint, Davies (1992) provides guiding principles that should be embodied in integrated curriculum development. They include:

1. Choose relevant topics, topics that will arouse curiosity and interest in students.
2. Convey clear goals and objectives to students. Students are more likely to feel that they learned if they know what the goals and objectives are.
3. Use a variety of topics, activities, and groupings, including individual work, presentations, interviews, writing, field trips, debates, movies, and small- and large-group activities.
4. Let students provide input and options for topics, projects, groupings.
5. Allow adequate time for students to work on and complete the activities.
6. Include both skill development and production of actual products in the unit.
7. Include field trips where students can experience a topic.
8. Use cooperative learning and other forms of group cooperation.
9. Have students share their knowledge and projects with others.
10. Involve parents and other community members in the unit.

The concepts of integrated curriculum and thematic instruction are by no means new. What is new is that we now know that such outcomes as the development of patterns and meaning, cooperative learning activities, and the emphasis on problem solving all have a neurobiological basis for enhanced learning. Thus, while the demands of creating such approaches to teaching and learning may be complex, the outcomes will have far-reaching benefits for the entire learning community.

SUMMARY

This chapter addressed the evolution of curriculum from the traditional, content-driven model to the constructivist and brain-based driven model. The integrated curriculum was emphasized as a mechanism, founded in brain-based research, that facilitates teaching-learning. While not considered an end in itself, the thematic approach to curriculum is a valuable way to address the differentiated learning needs of students, promote active student participation, and intellectually, physically, and emotionally connect students to the topics they are studying.

REFERENCES

Barab, Sasha A. and Anita Landa (1997). "Designing Effective Interdisciplinary Anchors." *Educational Leadership,* 54 (6), 52–55.

Beane, James A. (1995). *Toward a Coherent Curriculum. The 1995 ASCD Yearbook.* Alexandria, VA: Association for Supervision and Curriculum Development.

Brooks, Jacqueline Grennon and Martin G. Brooks. (1993). *The Case for Constructivist Classrooms.* Alexandria, VA: Association for Supervision and Curriculum Development.

Caine, Renate Nuemmella and Geoffrey Caine. (1997). *Unleashing the Power of Perceptual Change: The Potential of Brain-Based Learning.* Alexandria, VA: Association for Supervision and Curriculum Development.

———. (1991). *Teaching to the Brain.* Alexandria, VA: Association for Supervision and Curriculum Development. *Update Newsletter,* 33 (8), 1–3.

———. (1994). *Making Connections: Teaching and the Human Brain.* Alexandria, VA. Association for Supervision and Curriculum Development.

Cushman, Kathleen. (December, 1991). "Taking Stock: How Are Essential Schools Doing?" *Practitioner,* 18 (2).

Davies, M. A. (1992). "Are Interdisciplinary Units Worthwhile? Ask Students." In J. H. Lounsbury (Ed.). *Connecting the Curriculum Through Interdisciplinary Instruction.* Columbus, OH: National Middle School Association.

ERS: The Informed Educator Series. (1998). "Curriculum Integration." Arlington, VA: Educational Research Service.

Fogarty, Robin. (1997). *Brain Compatible Classrooms.* Arlington Heights, IL: Skylight Training and Publishing.

Fogarty, Robin and Judy Stoehr. (1995). *Integrating Curricula with Multiple Intelligences.* Arlington Heights, IL: IRI/Skylight Training and Publishing.

Germinario, Vito and Henry G. Cram. (1998). *Change for Public Education: Practical Strategies for the 21st Century,* Lancaster, PA: Technomic Publishing Company.

Jensen, Eric. (1995). *Brain-Based Learning and Teaching*. DelMar, CA: Turning Point Publishing.

————. (1998). *Teaching with the Brain in Mind*. Alexandria, VA: Association for Supervision and Curriculum Development.

Kovalik, Susan. (1994). *ITI: The Model: Integrated Thematic Instruction* (3d ed.). Kent, WA: Books for Educators.

Kovalik, Susan and Karen Olsen. (May, 1998). "How Emotions Run Us, Our Students and Our Classrooms." *NASSP Bulletin,* Reston, VA: National Association of Secondary School Principals. 82 (598), 29–37.

Lortre, D. C. (1975). *Schoolteacher: A Sociological Study*. Chicago, IL: University of Chicago Press.

Margulies, Nancy. (1991). *Mapping Inner Space: Learning and Teaching Mindmapping*. Tucson, AZ: Zephyr Press.

Maute, J. (1992). "Cross-Curricular Connections." In J. H. Lounsbury (ed.). *Connecting the Curriculum Through Interdisciplinary Instruction*. Columbus, OH: National Middle School Association.

Peters, Thomas. (1987). *Thriving on Chaos*. New York: Alfred A. Knopf.

Ross, Ann and Karen Olsen. (1993). "The Way We Were . . .The Way We Can Be: A Vision for the Middle School Through Integrated Thematic Instruction" (2d ed.). Kent, WA: Books for Educators, Covington Square.

Shoemaker, Betty Jean Eklund. (October, 1989). "Integrative Education. A Curriculum for the Twenty-First Century." *OSSC Bulletin* 33 (2), Eugene, OR: Oregon School Study Council. ED311602.

Shubert, William II. (1993). "Curriculum Reform." *Challenges and Achievements of American Education*. Alexandria, VA: The Association for Supervision and Curriculum Development, 80–84.

Sylwester, Robert. (1996). *A Celebration of Neurons: An Educator's Guide to the Human Brain*. Alexandria, VA: Association for Supervision and Curriculum Development.

Smith M. and J. O'Day. (1990). Position Paper on Education Reform Debate. Stanford University Center for Policy Resources in Education.

Uchida, Donna, Marion Cetron, and Floretta McKenzie. (1996). *Preparing Students for the Twenty-first Century*. Reston, VA: American Association of School Administrators.

Wells, Scott. (November, 1992). "Interdisciplinary Learning—Movement to Link Discipline Gains Momentum." Alexandria, VA: ASCD Curriculum Update.

Wurman, Richard Saul. (1989). *Information Anxiety*. New York: Doubleday.

CHAPTER 6

Professional Development

The key to successful innovation and change lies in our own growth and transformation, at least as much as, and probably more than, in any techniques or strategies we might seek to implement.

Renate Caine and Geoffrey Caine

The probability that the results of brain research will be applied in a school depends on its professional staff. Making teachers aware of and able to use our growing understanding of how the brain learns is dependent upon the effectiveness of the preservice and inservice training that teachers receive. Yet, despite the widespread interest and school district emphasis on professional development, there is still much to be learned about our new understanding of the brain that can be applied to teacher training. Germinario and Cram (1998) have identified several common elements that act as barriers to effective professional development:

- Activities are often centralized, with decisions made at the district level
- Presentations are "one-shot" experiences in which teachers sit passively while an "expert" trains them in new practices
- Professional development activities work independent of the norms, beliefs, and culture of the school
- Training opportunities don't utilize what is known about adult learning theory
- Professional development initiatives lack sustained commitment, investment, and resources

- Professional development initiatives lack school-based support and collaboration
- The system fails to provide recognition and rewards for professional growth

Brain research and past experience have clearly taught us that the development and maintenance of a skilled professional staff will require a new approach to what we have traditionally called professional development. What teachers are expected to give the student in a classroom is precisely what teachers fail to receive in their professional development experiences. Lieberman (1995) describes the similarities between student and teacher learning:

> People learn best through active involvement and through thinking about and becoming articulate about what they have learned. Processes, practices, and policies built on this view of learning are at the heart of a more expanded view of teacher development that encourages teachers to involve themselves as learners—in much the same way as they wish their students would (p. 592).

As classrooms should be organized to deliver instruction in a setting that is brain compatible, so too must professional development activities center around techniques and concepts associated with brain-based learning. In their most fundamental form, these techniques should include:

1. *Orchestrated immersion:* where teachers are immersed in meaningful experiences and are given ample opportunity to reflect upon what they have learned
2. *Relaxed alertness:* where teachers are engaged in a highly challenging environment while eliminating fear or threat for noncompliance
3. *Active processing:* which allows teachers the time and resources to consolidate, internalize, and integrate what they have learned into daily lessons and classroom practices (Caine and Caine, 1991)

CHARACTERISTICS OF BRAIN-BASED PROFESSIONAL DEVELOPMENT

We Learn What Is Personally Meaningful to Us

The content of professional development activities cannot be learned devoid of context and must have personal meaning and relevance. Initially, the brain's prior learning, or content schema, must be engaged in preparation to receive new knowledge. This must be focused in a content-specific location, with relevant connections to previous experiences and learning.

Additionally, the meaning of the content of professional development activities must be made clear so that real-world applications can be well understood.

The brain needs and automatically recognizes the familiar while simultaneously searching for a response to novel stimuli. Just as with the students they serve, adults in schools have a diversity of needs, interests, and developmental readiness when addressing new learning experiences. Thus, what may be meaningful to one teacher may not be relevant to another.

In planning for meaningful professional development experiences, we must be ever aware that one size, in fact, does not fit all. The needs and experience of an entry-level teacher would, by definition, be different from those of teachers who are in the advanced stages of career development. For example, an entry-level teacher who is experiencing difficulty in managing student behavior would find little relevance (or need) to engaging in training activities aimed at developing multimedia classroom presentations. Similarly, a skilled, experienced teacher would find little meaning in training sessions focusing on the basics of classroom management.

We Learn Best When Challenged with Achievable Goals

Caine and Caine (1991) suggest that the brain is like a camera lens. The brain's lens opens to receive information when interested and challenged, and closes when it perceives threat or imminent failure. Making maximum connections in the brain requires a combination of low threat and high challenge. Caine and Caine (1991) describe this phenomenon as "an optimal state of mind . . . combining moderate to high challenge that is built into intrinsic motivation with low threat and a pervasive sense of well-being" (p. 134). As discussed in chapter 3, the brain downshifts under threat (Hart, 1983). This produces a narrowing of our perceptional field, limiting our responses to new situations and lessening our ability to engage in complex tasks. In a professional development context, no clearer example exists than in areas related to technology training.

Anyone who has attended such training can easily "pick out" a beginner from among those who are more experienced in front of a computer. Confronted with the threat of failure and embarrassment in front of colleagues, a novice will often give up. This downshifting leads to teaching behaviors that follow one's existing beliefs and patterns while rationalizing why computers (and other technologies) really don't enhance learning experiences.

Adults have significant ego involvement in learning situations. Professional development activities must, therefore, be structured to provide recognition for the developmental readiness of the learner and to reduce the fear of failure or judgment during learning.

We Are Not Passive Recipients of Knowledge

Learning is an exceedingly complex phenomenon that engages our entire physiology. Learning is not externally directed but something that the learner must do for him/herself. The underlying principles of constructivism are built on a premise that (1) knowledge is constructed in the mind of the learner and (2) knowledge cannot be transferred intact from the mind of the teacher to the mind of the learner.

Thus, learners create their own knowledge structures rather than merely receiving them from others. From this perspective, knowledge is not transmitted from teacher to student, but instead is constructed in the mind of the learner. The implications of constructivism for professional development are far-reaching. Brooks and Brooks (1993) contend that in the absence of a constructivist setting, professional development programs would be trivialized.

What We Learn Is Influenced and Organized by Emotions

During the course of a learning experience, we don't learn only facts or practices. What we learn is significantly influenced and organized by our emotions and predetermined mindsets. Emotions and cognition cannot be separated and are critical to retention and memory, because they facilitate the storage and recall of information (Rosenfield, 1988).

While the relationship between emotions and learning is complex, people tend to learn more in an environment that is designed to:

- Provides meaning for what is learned
- Promotes success
- Is relatively free of stress

To facilitate such an environment in a professional development context, several conceptual and environmental factors must be carefully considered. One of the most significant of those factors is the maintenance of a *success orientation*. Professional development activities must be planned so that participants are able to find both meaning and success in all planned activities. If a participant believes he/she cannot accomplish a task or master a concept, then he/she will "downshift" to a point where the emotional tension will severely limit the ability to be successful. Senge (1990) suggests that negative emotions have the effect of lowering the vision for what is success. That in turn prompts a negative predisposition concerning the value of the experience itself.

The Emotional Climate

The brain is a social brain (Caine and Caine, 1997). Most learning takes place within a social context that is being influenced by social interactions. Thus, participants engaged in professional development activities must be *actively involved* with their colleagues so that they can share, reflect, and generalize their learning and experiences. Through this involvement, individuals receive critical feedback regarding the relevance and utility of their thoughts and actions. In planning for learning experiences, close attention must be paid to the social setting.

Careful consideration should be given to the establishment of an emotional climate where participants can safely *express positive or negative emotions*. The climate must be "emotionally safe," one in which the contributions of all participants are valued and appreciated.

Finally, professional development experiences should be approached with genuine *enthusiasm*. Regardless of the nature of the professional development experiences or the expertise of the participants, much is to be gained by maintaining a positive perspective and high expectations. This enthusiasm and positive modeling facilitates attention and meaning and sends both conscious and unconscious signals regarding the importance and value of what is being learned.

Emotion and the Total Environment

Because learning involves both focused attention and peripheral perception, it is influenced by environmental factors (Caine and Caine, 1997). The brain absorbs information both when paying attention and from signals that are outside the field of immediate attention.

One cannot overlook or minimize the importance of the where, when, and how associated with professional development activities. An attractive, safe, and comfortable environment must be maintained. If activities are directive, that is, participants are engaged in presentations or group-related activities, then the setting should be away from the distractions of their classroom or workstation. The facilities should be pleasant and attractive, thereby adding to the value and importance of the experience.

Additionally, the timing of the experience is critical. Being rushed or scheduling activities at a time when the participants believe they should be somewhere else (i.e., with students or during an important school event) will lessen the likelihood of maintaining focused attention and a positive feeling.

The concepts and strategies that are provided form the context by which professional development can become more brain friendly. Speck (1996) provides an additional list of considerations when designing brain-compatible professional development experiences:

- Adults will commit to learning when the goals and objectives are considered realistic and important to them. Application in the "real world" is important and relevant to the adult learner's personal and professional needs.
- Adults want to be the origin of their own learning and will resist

learning activities they believe are an attack on their competence. Thus, professional development needs to give participants some control over the what, who, how, why, when, and where of their learning.

- Adult learners need to see that the professional development learning and their day-to-day activities and problems are related and relevant.

- Adult learners need direct concrete experiences, in which they apply the learning in real work.

- Adult learning has ego involvement. Professional development must be structured to provide support from peers and to reduce the fear of judgment during learning.

- Adults need to receive feedback on how they are doing and the results of their efforts. Opportunities must be built into professional development activities that allow the learner to practice the learning and receive structured, helpful feedback.

- Adults need to participate in small-group activities during the learning to move them beyond understanding to application, analysis, synthesis, and evaluation. Small-group activities provide an opportunity to share, reflect, and generalize their learning and experience.

- Adult learners come to learning with a wide range of previous experiences, knowledge, self-direction, interests, and competencies. This diversity must be accommodated in the professional development planning.

- Transfer of learning for adults is not automatic and must be facilitated. Coaching and other kinds of follow-up support are needed to help adult learners transfer learning into daily practice so that it is sustained.

A DIFFERENTIATED MODEL FOR PROFESSIONAL DEVELOPMENT

In many respects, teacher training and professional development must be reconceptualized to meet the needs of the teacher from entry into the profession, to advanced stages of development, and finally to a point where he/she is recognized as competent and proficient. Each teacher has a novel brain and different needs as he or she relates to professional growth and development. Each brings a different set of expectations as to the utility of staff and professional development activities. Finally, each derives distinctly different benefits from generic inservice training as well as through self-initiated classroom problem-solving research.

Glickman (1990) expands upon this concept by adding a dimension concerned with human development and differences. This dimension encourages the selection of professional development activities that allow the greatest growth potential for each teacher. This developmental approach is based on three general propositions.

First, teachers (and other professionals) operate at different levels of professional development. They vary in how they view and relate to themselves, students, and others. They differ in their abilities to analyze instructional problems, to use a repertoire of problem-solving strategies, and to match appropriate strategies to particular situations. Furthermore, the same teacher may vary depending on the particular instructional topic or timing of life and work events.

Second, teachers operate at differing levels of conceptual understanding, ability, and effectiveness. Teachers at lower developmental levels need less structure and a more active role in decision making.

Third, the long-range goal of professional development should be to increase every teacher's ability to grow into higher stages of thought. Glickman suggests that more reflective, self-directed teachers will be better able to solve their own instructional problems and meet their students' educational needs.

A differentiated method for the professional development of staff, addresses many of the propositions related to the application of brain-based learning are addressed. First, the activity becomes personally meaningful, with activities directly related to the perceived needs and/or developmental readiness of the participant. Second, the experience can be made challenging while focusing on achievable goals that are consistent with the skills and experience of the participant. Third, participants need not be relegated to the role of passive recipient of information, since each will engage in activities that can be easily integrated into an existing set of skills and experiences. Finally, critical issues related to emotions in a learning situation are more easily managed by promot-

Beginner 1–3 years	Advance Beginner/ Competent 3–5 years	Skilled/Experienced Career
Probationary	Developmental	Self-initiated Growth
1. Induction	1. Two classroom observations focused around predetermined instructional phenomenon	1. Classroom observations only if required by state law or district policy
2. Knowledge Instructional model		2. Action research
3. 4–6 classroom observations	2. Instructional innovations, cooperative learning, technology, etc.	
4. Mentor/coach		
5. Artifact collection	3. Peer coaching	
6. Journal (diary)		
7. Discussion groups: on-going reflective activities		

Figure 6.1

ing a learning climate that is more likely to lead to success, thus minimizing both stress and downshifting.

An essential component of this type of model is that through appropriate activities and professional opportunities at each developmental level, teachers would be able to think in a reflective manner and become increasingly more responsible for their own supervision and professional growth. Figure 6.1 (Germinario and Cram, 1998) illustrates the nature of a brain-compatible developmental (differentiated) model that provides specific activities that are appropriate for professional development within each teacher developmental stage. This model provides for a differential treatment of professional development and supervisory behaviors based on the individual needs of the teacher and the organizational demands of the school. Additionally, the model reflects the need for professional development to be personally meaningful and appropriately challenging and to provide for active participation of the teacher in his/her professional growth.

Unlike existing systems, differentiated practices discriminate between the need for knowledge acquisition and detailed accountability of probationary teachers and the need to stimulate professional development for experienced teachers. The model moves from direct supervisory assistance and monitoring toward increasing nondirective applications, emphasizing self-initiated growth through reflection and problem solving, ultimately giving the teachers increasing control and responsibility for their own professional growth.

THE BEGINNING TEACHER

Few things in education are more difficult than one's first year as a teacher. The research on new-teacher attrition is dramatic:

- Almost 15 percent of new teachers leave teaching after one year.
- Between 40 percent and 50 percent of new teachers leave in fewer than seven years.
- As a group, the most academically talented teachers are the least likely to stay in the profession.
- Young teachers, when compared with more experienced teachers, report more emotional exhaustion and a greater degree of depersonalization (Tonnensen and Patterson, 1992).

Beginning teachers are expected to come into the classroom equipped with the skills that can promote classroom management and active student learning. All too often the novice teacher comes into the profession with a mental model that guides his/her beliefs, images, assumptions, and actions built on a very limited experiential and conceptual framework. Essentially, the most prominent factors that influence teachers' mental models include the teachers they encountered during their own education, a brief period of student/practice teaching, and a somewhat superficial exposure to the science of teaching while in a teacher preparation program. Thus, the emphasis in professional development for novice teachers should be on the creation or requirement of a mental model for effective teaching that is based on what we now know about the brain.

Their professional development should emphasize the skills associated with brain-based classroom management and brain-compatible instructional delivery. Specifically, ongoing opportunities for training and discussion in areas related to (1) instructional modeling, (2) the development of classroom routine and procedures, (3) an analysis of teaching artifacts, (4) time for self-reflection through the keeping of a journal, and (5) direct classroom observations should provide the foundation for successful induction into the teaching profession (Germinario and Cram, 1998), thus providing activities that are personally meaningful and challenging to them in their early experiences as teachers.

Providing such activities ensures that the training experiences and personally meaningful, achievable outcomes are conducted within a context that emphasizes standards for success. While the activities are somewhat directive, they allow the beginning teacher to construct a mental image of effective teaching strategies and behaviors within predetermined parameters. Importantly, the novice teacher is encouraged to actively participate within the context consistent with his or her professional growth needs. Ultimately, it is these parameters, based on research and effective practices, that will form the foundation for a successful beginning teaching experience.

THE ADVANCED BEGINNING/COMPETENT TEACHER

As a teacher begins to conceptualize and, ultimately, effectively utilize basic brain-based models of instruction, his/her needs for professional growth become increasingly more sophisticated. With an established mental model of the rudiments of effective teaching, the advanced/competent teacher has internalized principles and practices that guide his/her actions. The more meaningful and challenging goal of professional development for teachers in this stage should be the development of deeper meaning that patterns the application of teaching strategies. Confronted with new strategies or techniques, teachers must choose those that fit their mental model while ensuring the dignity of what they already do. Thus, professional development for a teacher at the competent developmental stage must focus on helping the teacher internalize, reshape, and transform new information. This transformation occurs through the creation of new understandings.

Joyce and Showers (1988) identified five essential elements to be included in professional development activities to help transfer a concept or strategy into a teacher's delivery system. They suggest that teachers need:

- To study the theory and rationale for the new practice
- An opportunity to see the new strategy demonstrated
- An opportunity to practice under simulated conditions
- Feedback about performance
- Coaching by colleagues to provide support, technical feedback, and mutual problem-solving opportunities as the new strategy is implemented

Intuitively, Joyce and Showers have created a brain-compatible staff development strategy that addresses the cognitive and emotional requirements of adult learning.

As teachers develop confidence through their successful teaching experiences, they have increasingly more opportunities to interact with their colleagues on issues related to school life. These interactions provide a vehicle for social support as well as a mechanism to discuss, and derive meaning for, the complex dynamics of the classroom.

Given the increasing social and emotional context of the competent teacher's professional life, it is important that professional development activities provide the time and the framework for collegial partnerships. The most common method to accomplish this goal is through *peer coaching*.

Simply stated, "peer coaching is the process where teams of teachers regularly observe one another and provide support, companionship, feedback, and assistance" (Valencia and Killian, 1988, p. 170). Identifying peer coaching as a major component of staff development, Joyce and Showers (1981) outlined the four functions of the coaching process as (1) the provision of companionship, (2) the provision of technical feedback, (3) the analysis of application (attaining "deep" meaning), and (4) adaptation to students.

The idea of encouraging school staff members to work as collaborative partners is based on the assumption that teacher and school improvement are most effectively promoted within the school environment. Research on instructionally effective schools has suggested that in the most successful schools, staff members are likely to:

- Discuss teaching and learning with one another
- Critique each other's work
- Collaborate on the preparation of materials
- Jointly design meaningful learning experiences (Little, 1986)

All of these activities are natural processes in the brain's functioning and are consistent with adult learning theory.

Peer coaching is a brain-compatible strategy for improving teachers' instructional skills and promoting professional growth. This is accomplished within a brain-friendly context. This context permits teachers to engage in activities that have personal meaning and relevance to what goes on within their classrooms. Further, it makes them active participants in the construction of new understandings about classroom life and student learning. Finally, it provides a safe, supported emotional environment in which to share and grow.

THE SKILLED, EXPERIENCED TEACHER

Skilled, experienced teachers, by and large, need to construct their own mental models as to the direction and scope of their professional development. In this role, they need to engage in investigations concerning how best to solve problems related to their classrooms and students.

There is growing support that research by teachers into their own classrooms and practices can function as a powerful means of professional development and also can contribute to the knowledge base in education (Goswani and Stillman, 1987). To that end, brain-compatible professional development for the skilled, experienced teacher should be focused upon the creation of compelling experiences that are challenging and meaningful. Activities are most productive when teachers are *immersed* in real-life experiences or problems that require active processing of their skills.

This solution-oriented activity conducted by an individual or a group of teachers is often called *action research*. Action research is characterized by spiraling cycles of problem identification, systematic data collection, reflection, analysis, data-driven action taken, and problem redefinition. The linking of the words *action* and *research* highlights the essential features of this method: trying out ideas in practice as a means of increasing knowledge about and/or improving curriculum, teaching, and learning (Kemmis and McTaggart, 1982).

Most often, action research is a collaborative activity whose practitioners work together to help one another design and carry out investigations in their classrooms. When conducted by teams of teachers, the process enables them to: (1) improve student learning, (2) improve their own practice, (3) contribute to their own profession, and (4) overcome the isolation commonly experienced by classroom teachers (Sagor, 1992).

Within this context, action research becomes a strategy for orchestrated immersion of the skilled, experienced teacher into multiple, complex, authentic experiences. Total immersion is one of the essential elements of brain-compatible learning. When engaged in such relevant, complex problem solving, the teacher is forced to look at student learning as an integrative, complex phenomenon. In effect, immersion induces the teacher to process globally and not in a purely segmented, brick-building fashion (Caine and Caine, 1991).

The benefits of action research have been reported by teachers from kindergarten through twelfth grade (Johnson, 1993). Goswani and Stillman (1987) cite important changes that occur when teachers conduct action research. The authors assert that teachers who conduct research maintain a theoretical perspective that find connections with practice. These teachers' self-perceptions are enhanced, and they become professionally more active. These teachers begin to observe students more closely and learn about new ways to promote success. They develop into users of current literature and research, becoming more evaluative of curricular material and methods. They are able to study learning and report their findings in practical, inexpensive ways. Finally, they believe that teachers who collaborate with students in classroom research help learners achieve at higher levels.

The underlying success of action research as a professional developmental tool may rest on the constructivist nature of the activity. First, classrooms become learning environments where teachers search for meaning, appreciate uncertainty, and inquire in a systematic fashion. Second, action research shifts the teacher's role from that of passive recipient of knowledge to one that encourages collaborative thinking, demonstration, and problem solving. Third, teachers begin to structure classroom activity and learning around primary concepts, not isolated parts. Finally, action research tends to link the learner with the teacher, providing nonjudgmental feedback in an environment that can be assessed while learning is still occurring.

Simply stated, this constructivist framework creates an environment in which teachers are encouraged to find deep meaning in their actions by thinking and exploring. Yet "teacher as researcher" will likely be a new concept for even the most experienced teacher. It becomes critical that consideration be given to the emotional environment needed for teachers to feel secure in their expanded role. Bennett (1993) found that teachers who worked in environments that supported collaboration and research reported that the following conditions aided them in sustaining their role:

- Administrators demonstrated a strong interest in educational research and expected teachers to be familiar with recent literature.
- Administrators openly encouraged teachers to test and implement new research findings in the classroom.
- District newsletters provided teachers with updates on educational research.
- School libraries provided teacher resource centers that included research journals and educational books.
- The district encouraged teachers to attend conferences and seminars and paid their fees.
- Teachers were encouraged to participate in a degree program that provided formal research training.
- Teachers had ongoing opportunities to reflect on classroom practices and share information.

Research emerging from practice has a natural place in schools. When the research is conducted by skilled, trained teachers, the research questions are more relevant, the investigation more natural, and the findings more credible and practical for classroom practice. The outcome of this activity will provide a vehicle to effectively address the developmental professional needs of the skilled, experienced teacher. This is accomplished by creating an environment for orchestrated immersion, an environment that challenges teachers to become more self-directed in the identification of how they can solve complex, student-centered problems that exist within the "real life" of their classrooms.

DIFFERENTIATED TEACHER PORTFOLIOS—A TOOL FOR ONGOING ASSESSMENT

Much research has indicated the direct link between quality professional growth opportunities for teachers and a wide variety of positive outcomes related to student learning and successful schools. Asayesh (1993) has summarized the research and concluded that:

1. It is one of three essential ingredients of successful school improvement. The two others are a supportive institutional context and strong content.
2. It employs strategies that are research-based, meaning they have proven to be effective.
3. It is an ongoing process beginning with intensive training but continuing on the job site. Follow-up and support activities should be built into the school's or school system's institutional structure.
4. It will make a difference in student learning, improving outcomes ranging from attendance to grades.
5. It will include an evaluation component that measures effectiveness in terms of both implementation and student outcomes. This information can demonstrate progress and serve as a blueprint for modifications.
6. The staff developers practice what they preach, maintaining an attitude of openness to change and personal growth.
7. Opportunities for collaboration and joint planning are built in.
8. Teachers and other staff are involved in their own growth and take ownership of the program.

Yet, as with all other classroom and organizational initiatives, care must be taken to provide an ongoing *assessment* of the utility of a school's/district's professional development initiatives. Unfortunately, much of what is important to the brain, that which truly shapes our understanding, our thinking, and our behaviors, is difficult to assess. Typical methods of evaluating teacher and professional growth, regardless of developmental level, are all too often reduced to brief site visits by the principal to observe the interplay between students and teachers. While having some limited value, relying on a brief "snapshot" of classroom life fails to meaningfully assess the extent to which teachers have learned and integrated strategies that address the complexities of teaching and student learning. Jensen (1995) provides seven categories to describe the ways in which the human brain can evidence learning:

1. As *data or information:* The learner replays information without making relevant connections. In a professional development context, for example, a novice teacher may be asked to name the components of the district instructional model.
2. As *meaning:* Information is transformed by the learner's discovering patterns and relationships. Here the novice teacher can express understanding by planning and demonstrating the steps in an effective lesson.
3. As a *new or better working model:* A system is consciously or unconsciously developed that organizes principles into how something works. In this instance the novice teacher begins to see patterns, such as the relationships of the teaching model to its effect on students.
4. *Specific, useful "how to" strategies:* Skills are embedded as procedural memory (processes that have been practiced to the extent that they have become automatic). Here the novice teacher can routinely deliver lessons that reflect the concepts embodied in the district's instructional model.
5. *Attitudes:* This involves the perceptual bias and opinions that change one's feelings about a topic. In this case the novice teacher begins to internalize and reflect upon the utility of the instructional strategies he/she is emphasizing. In short, a mental image begins to develop about the behaviors that constitute good teaching.
6. *Observable behavior and changes:* This refers to a change in physical behavior that demonstrates that, biologically, something has been learned. The novice teacher now consistently demonstrates the characteristics, skills, and behaviors deemed appropriate for a professional at his/her professional growth stage.

7. *Internal:* This involves a demonstration of how learning affects someone personally and also the implications for one's past, present, and future. The novice teacher has now internalized all the features established for success at his/her professional stage and is developmentally ready to take increasing responsibility for his/her own professional growth.

An emerging method that capitalizes on concepts related to constructivism and brain compatibility is the development of a *professional portfolio.* A professional portfolio is an accumulation of personal data about an individual teacher. The folder can include a record of achievement; samples of work; observations made by a supervisor, a colleague, or oneself; and parent and/or student comments or evaluations. A portfolio can help strengthen a faculty member's overall organization, demonstrate progress and innovative work, and provide information that helps improve the performance and quality of the overall program (Perkins and Gelfer, 1993).

On a simplistic level, a teacher's portfolio can be seen as a container for storing and displaying evidence of that teacher's knowledge, skills, and accomplishments. Yet, on a conceptual level, a portfolio also embodies an attitude that assessment is dynamic and that the portrayals of teacher performance are based on multiple sources of evidence collected over time in authentic settings (Valencia, McGinley, and Pearson, 1990).

Creating a professional portfolio can benefit a teacher in many of the same ways that teachers have observed portfolios benefiting students. The portfolio helps identify the teacher's best work or practices, prompts self-reflection and analysis, provides the basis for dialogue, and forms the foundation for self-assessment.

The content of the professional portfolio should vary along a continuum providing for differences among the professional development activities of the probationary teacher, the advanced beginner/competent teacher, and the skilled, experienced teacher (Germinario and Cram, 1998).

For the *probationary teacher,* the portfolio should include evidence of attainment of baseline competencies and standards. Consistent with figure 6.1, entries into the probationary teacher's portfolio would include selected artifacts, classroom observation reports, indicators of successful induction into the school, selected lesson plans, and evidence of ongoing reflection and professional development consistent with his/her developmental needs.

Since baseline competencies can be assured, the professional portfolio for the advanced beginner/competent teacher should include evidence of higher levels of abstraction. While classroom observation reports may still be appropriate as evidence of mastery of school instructional expectations, entries showing evidence of more innovative classroom techniques and professional development must be used as a standard for teachers in this stage of readiness. Of particular importance is the inclusion of evidence of collegiality and experimentation.

Little (1981), in studying the norms and work conditions that appear to cultivate collegiality and experimentation, describes four conditions that could be included in the competent teacher's portfolio. These conditions, in reality, are brain compatible, in that they are focused on the central themes of orchestrated immersion, relaxed alertness, and active processing.

1. Teachers engage in frequent, continuous and increasingly concrete and precise *talk* about teaching practice (as distinct from teacher characteristics and failings, the social lives of teachers, etc.) By such talk, teachers build up a shared language adequate to the complexity of teaching, capable of distinguishing one practice and its virtue from another.

2. Teachers frequently *observe* each other teaching, and provide each other with useful (if potentially frightening) evaluations of their teaching. Only such observation and feedback can provide shared *referents* for the shared language of teaching, and both demand and provide the precision and concreteness that makes the talk about teaching useful.

3. Teachers *plan, design, research, evaluate,* and *prepare teaching materials together.* The most prescient observations remain academic ("just theory") without the machinery to act on them. By joint work on materials, teachers and administrators share the considerable burden of development required by long-term improvement . . . and make rising standards for their work attainable by them and by their students.

4. Teachers *teach each other* the practice of teaching.

Finally, the portfolio of the *skilled, experienced* teacher should include evidence of self-directed professional growth. The teacher in this developmental stage should report on the purpose and outcomes of his/her action research project. This report should include a statement of the problem being investigated, a review of relevant research, the nature of the classroom experimentation, the standards used in measuring outcomes, and, finally, a discussion of how the project has influenced or will influence classroom practice.

SUMMARY

This chapter described the elements associated with effective professional development as it relates to adult learning and brain functioning. Specifically, it emphasized the constructivist perspective while recognizing the differentiated needs and readiness levels of teachers.

Sparks and Hirsh (1997) suggest that if the promising constructivist goals of active, mind-engaging learning and deep understanding are to be widely practiced in the classroom, then both teachers and administrators need to practice these behaviors in their own professional development activities. Elaborating on a new vision for staff development, Sparks and Hirsh propose that:

> Rather than receiving "knowledge" from "experts" in training sessions, teachers and administrators will collaborate with peers, researchers, and their own students to make sense of the teaching/learning process in their own contexts. Staff development from a constructivist perspective will include activities such as action research, conversations with peers about the beliefs and assumptions that guide their instruction, and reflective practices such as journal keeping—activities that many educators may not even view as staff development (p. 55).

Professional development activities should model the concepts and strategies related to what we know about adult learning and brain-compatible teaching. This must be a dynamic process that progressively weans teachers from their dependence on procedural knowledge and practices to the point where they have confidence to manage their own professional growth.

It will be only through a conscious effort to provide brain-friendly staff development that we can expect teachers to translate brain research into classroom application.

REFERENCES

Asayesh, Belareh. (1993). "Staff Development for Improving Student Outcomes." *Journal of Staff Development,* 14 (3), 24–27.

Bennett, C. R. (1993). "Teacher-Researcher: All Dressed Up and No Place to Go?" *Educational Leadership,* 51 (10), 69–70.

Brooks, J. and M. Brooks. (1993). *The Case for Constructivist Classrooms.* Alexandria, VA: Association for Supervision and Curriculum Development.

Caine, Renate N. and Geoffrey Caine. (1991). *Making Connections: Teaching and the Human Brain.* Alexandria, VA: Association for Supervision and Curriculum Development.

———. (1997). *Education on the Edge of Possibility.* Alexandria, VA: Association for Supervision and Curriculum Development.

Germinario, Vito and Henry G. Cram. (1998). *Change for Public Education: Practical Approaches for the 21st Century.* Lancaster, PA: Technomic Publishing Company.

Glickman, Carl D. (1990). *Supervision of Instruction: A Developmental Approach.* 2d ed. Needham Heights, MA: Allyn and Bacon.

Goswani, Dixie and Peter Stillman. (1987). *Reclaiming the Classroom: Teacher Research as an Agency for Change.* Upper Montclair, NJ: Boynton Cook.

Greenwald, R., L. V. Hedges, and R. D. Laine. (1996). "The Effect of School Resources on Student Achievement." *Review of Education Research,* 66 (3), 361–396.

Hart, L. (1983). "Constructivism: A Theory of Knowledge." *Journal of Clinical Education,* 63 (10), 873–878.

Jensen, Eric. (1995). *Brain-based Learning and Teaching.* DelMar, CA: Turning Point Publishing.

Johnson, R. W. (1993). "Where Can Teacher Research Lead? One Teacher's Day Dream." *Educational Leadership,* 50 (9), 66–68.

Joyce, Bruce and Beverly Showers. (1981). "Transfer of Training: The Contribution of Coaching." *Boston University Journal of Education,* 1 (2), 163–172.

———. (1988). *Student Achievement Through Staff Development.* White Plains, NJ: Longman.

Kemmis, S. and R. McTaggart. (1982). *The Action Research Planner.* Victoria, Australia: Deakin University Press.

Lieberman, A. (1995). "Practices That Support Teacher Development." *Phi Delta Kappan,* 76 (8), 591–596.

Little, Judith W. (1981). "The Power of Organizational Setting: School Norms and Staff Development." Paper presented at the annual meeting of the American Educational Research Association, Los Angeles, CA.

————. (1982). "Norms of Collegiality and Experimentation: Workplace Conditions of School Success." *American Educational Research Journal,* 19 (3), 325–340.

Perkins, Peggy G. and Jeffrey I. Gelfer. (1993). "Portfolio Assessment for Teachers." *The Clearing House,* 66 (4), 235–237.

Rosenfield, I. (1988). *The Invention of Memory.* New York: Basic Books.

Sagor, Richard. (1992). *How to Conduct Collaborative Action Research.* Alexandria, VA: Association for Supervision and Curriculum Development.

Senge, Peter M. (1990). *The Fifth Discipline.* New York: Doubleday.

Sparks, Dennis and Stephanie Hirsh. (1997). *A New Vision for Staff Development.* Alexandria, VA: Association for Supervision and Curriculum Development.

Speck, Marsha. (1996). "Best Practices in Professional Development." *ERS Spectrum,* 14 (2), 33–41.

Tonnensen, Sandra and Susan Patterson. (1992). "Fighting the First-Year Jitters." *The Executive Educator,* 14 (1), 29–30.

Valencia, S. W. and J. P. Killian. (1988). "Overcoming Obstacles to Teacher Change: Direction from School-Based Efforts." *Journal of Staff Development,* 9 (2), 168–174.

Valencia, Sheila, William McGinley, and P. David Pearson. (1990). "Assessing Reading and Writing: Building a More Complete Picture." In *Reading in the Middle School,* 2d ed., edited by Gerald Duffy. Newark, DE: International Reading Association.

CHAPTER 7

Brain-Friendly School Organization and Climate

I don't only use all the brains that I have, but all that I can borrow.

Woodrow Wilson

For a school to be successful it must be a community of professionals working toward a vision of teaching and learning that transcends individual classrooms, grade levels, and departments. In short, the entire school community must develop a covenant to guide future decisions about goals and operation of the school (Glickman, 1992). While it would be difficult to take issue with the need for a shared school covenant, the realities of how schools are currently organized and how they operate make this goal unlikely. The problem lies in the way teachers have, or in reality have not, been engaged as active stakeholders in school life. Teaching is essentially a very lonely profession. Teachers spend almost their entire day with children. Their evenings are often spent grading papers and developing lesson plans. Teachers clearly know about their classroom, and they may know something about what's going on in their school, but most likely they don't know much about the goals of the system of which they are a part.

The problem lies, to a great extent, in that what we know about brain compatibility within the context of classroom teaching and learning is not translated to or utilized in the way we organize or operate our schools. While we have become increasingly aware of the need to create learning organization for children, little attention has been given to establishing those same characteristics for the adults within the school.

141

Senge (1990) contends that it is no accident that most organizations grow and learn poorly. He suggests that the way they are designed and managed, the way people's jobs are defined, and, most importantly, the way we all have been taught to think and interact create fundamental "learning disabilities." He identifies seven such learning disabilities:

1. *I Am My Own Position.* We are trained to be loyal to our position to a point where we confuse it with our identity. By focusing on our own position, little thought for the activities or responsibility for the results of the entire organization is internalized.

   In schools, teachers are much more concerned about "my students," "my curriculum," etc. than they may ever be about school achievement levels, school climate, or the mission of the school or district.

2. *The Enemy Is Out There.* There is a propensity to find someone or something outside ourselves to blame when things go wrong. As a by-product of "I am my position," we tend not to see how our own actions extend beyond the boundary of that position.

   All too often teachers blame their lack of success on issues they perceive having little control over, such as permissive promotion policies, lack of resources, and lack of administrative support.

3. *The Illusion of Taking Charge.* Senge suggests that this perceived aggressive action against an external enemy or event, this proactiveness, is actually reactiveness in disguise. True proactiveness comes instead from seeing how we contribute to our own problems.

   Not given adequate knowledge of the totality of an issue or event, teachers tend to go about reacting to a problem in isolation. These independent actions do little to facilitate good for the entire school. For example, sensing increased problems related to class discipline, a teacher may develop a set of class rules and consequences. These rules may, in fact, be quite different from those established for his/her students when they go, for example, to physical education or music class.

4. *The Fixation on Events.* Organizations are dominated by concern with events. While the events may be significant, they tend to distract us from seeing the long-term patterns of change that lie behind the events and from understanding the causes of those patterns.

Critical events, such as acts of violence or drug abuse in the school, typically generate a series of policies, rules, and regulations to combat the effects of such disruptive or destructive behavior. Often fixated on the event and the lack of time and organizational facility for meaningful reflection and collaboration, school personnel fail to generate the learning necessary to attack the underlying causes of the behaviors.

5. *The Parable of the Boiled Frog.* This parable is built on the premise that if you place a frog in a pot of boiling water it will immediately try to scramble out. But if you place the frog in room-temperature water, it will stay put. As the temperature gradually rises, the frog will become increasingly lethargic until eventually it boils.

    As in other organizations, real threats to schooling don't come from sudden events but from gradual, often slow processes. Change in student behavior within a classroom or school is not predicated on a single event. Instead, it develops in time as a result of our inability to slow down and pay attention to the subtleties of daily school life.

6. *The Delusion of Learning from Experience.* Experience is unquestionably a powerful determinant of learning. Though we learn from experience, we never directly experience the consequences of many of our most important decisions.

    In schools, teachers' vision is limited in time to the year they may have a student in their classroom. Given this relatively short "learning horizon," it becomes nearly impossible to truly learn the consequences from direct experience. Again in our example of student misbehavior, a teacher will never really know if the experiences associated with the establishment of classroom rules and consequences had any long-lasting effect on how a student behaves as he/she progresses through the grades or to adulthood.

7. *The Myth of the Management Team.* In response to these dilemmas and disabilities, management teams are often formed. Representing different functions and areas of expertise, these teams are supposed to solve complex issues critical to the life of the organization. All too often, however, teams spend their time fighting for turf, making compromises, and dealing with management's inherent uneasiness with the threat of shared power. Argyris (1990) describes this process as blocking out new understandings that may threaten us. The consequence is charac-

terized as "skilled incompetence"—teams are full of people who are incredibly proficient at keeping themselves from learning.

School-based planning/improvement teams are a now common feature in schools across the country. Yet little evidence can be found to link their activities to systemic school reform or increased levels of student achievement. Turf battles, the imposition of managerial prerogatives, and the lack of a clearly defined purpose have often led to the demise of a potentially important way to immerse teachers in all aspects of school life and decision making.

THE CHARACTERISTICS OF A LEARNING ORGANIZATION

A learning organization is one in which people at all levels, individually and collectively, are continually increasing their capacity to produce results that have personal meaning and that they truly care about. In an organization that values learning, its members must realize that all smaller parts within the organization comprise a larger system. In most cases this larger, more complex system has capabilities that the smaller system lacks. For example, the brain is made up of individual neurons that, when functioning together, have the capacity to perform tasks no single neuron can perform alone. These new capabilities can only be realized when the neurons are working together.

To become true learning organizations, schools must adopt principles associated with *systems thinking*. Senge (1990) defines systems thinking as an examination, within an organization, of the individual patterns that connect to the larger system. Instead of focusing on improving individual components of an organization (school), systems thinking focuses on the interconnectedness of all things and recognizes that change is not always rational or linear.

While traditional models of change are rooted in stability, rationality, and structure, systems thinking assumes a more unpredictable, dynamic view of organizational change. Evans (1996) has discussed the distinctions between these two models of change; these are summarized in table 7.1.

Learning organizations have the capacity for continual improvement. These organizations develop a culture that initiates innovation by recognizing and accepting what is good, but they are secure enough to cre-

Table 7.1   Paradigms of Change

	Rational-Structural	*Strategic-Systemic*
Environment	Stable predictable	Turbulent unpredictable
Organization	Stable logical	Fluid psychological
Planning	Objective, linear long-range	Pragmatic, adaptable medium range
Innovation	Product fixed outcome	Process emerging outcome
Focus	Structure, function tasks, roles, rules	People, culture meaning, motivation
Implementation	Almost purely top-down disseminating, pressuring	Top-down and bottom-up commitment-building

ate a productive level of dissatisfaction that essentially says, "We can do better" (Ogden and Germinario, 1995).

Senge (1990) describes five characteristics of a learning organization. In addition to systems thinking, traits that cultivate and sustain an effective learning environment include:

- *Personal Mastery*—This is a continuing process of clarifying and deepening one's personal vision, a focus of energies, an increased capacity for patience and a greater capability for seeing reality objectively. In short, Senge believes that "an organization's commitment to and capacity for learning can be no greater than that of its members" (p. 7).
- *Mental Models*—These are deeply engrained assumptions, generalizations, or even pictures or images that influence how we comprehend and react to the world. Learning organizations find and systematize ways to bring people together to develop the best possible mental models for facing any situation at hand (p. 181).
- *Building Shared Vision*—This develops when the members of an organization collectively develop a "picture of the future" (p. 9). Shared vision, then, is the focusing of the personal visions of all orga-

nizational members. As with a personal vision, a shared vision creates a mental model that people throughout the organization carry.

- *Team Learning*—This refers to the ability of a group of people to suspend their assumptions and freely think together. This involves dialogue among members of the group to create meaning. Just like a complex system, collective results that are greater than the sum of their parts will emerge.

THE COMPLEXITIES OF CHANGE

Resistance to change, in one form or another, has been a common theme in education. Resistance to educational change manifests itself most frequently in relation to policy or curriculum innovations. Typically, the resistance comes from teachers on whom the change has the greatest impact. Interestingly, a corollary of change is the (almost) overwhelming desire of individuals to maintain the status quo. Both formal and informal influences exist to preserve the traditional ways of thinking and acting, as well as the roles and functions of staff members within the school. In a very real way, change upsets the balance and order that have been institutionalized over varying lengths of time. The resistance to individual and organizational change can manifest itself in both subtle and not-so-subtle ways. The behaviors range from illusions of support without substance, to manipulative behaviors, to outright refusal to cooperate. Regardless of the indicators of resistance, it is imperative to understand that with the introduction of change will come a certain degree of dissonance. If schools are to change into learning organizations, major stakeholders in the schools must plan for the dynamics inherent in the change process (Germinario and Cram, 1998).

The key factors in change are what it means to those who must implement it and that its primary meanings encourage resistance. Evans (1996) describes four characteristics embodied in this resistance:

1. *Change Provokes Loss.* Things that we know and use are rooted in feelings that have emotional significance. Significant change means loss of what is valued and causes a kind of bereavement.
2. *Change Challenges Competency.* Alterations in practices and pro-

cedures hamper the ability of teachers to perform their jobs confidently and successfully, making them feel inadequate and insecure.

3. *Change Creates Confusion.* Change increases unpredictability. Change upsets the coherence of organizational design, clarity, and appropriateness of formal roles, rules, and policies.

4. *Change Causes Conflict.* Change almost always generates friction, both between individuals and between groups. This phenomenon is promoted by the notion that change invariably, especially at first, produces winners and losers.

While various strategies have proven successful, there are common themes that cultivate successful change in schools. Primary to this success is the creation of a professional culture in which decisions to change are based on informed research, support, inquiry, consultation, and collaboration. Additionally, just as classrooms are to be organized and operated to facilitate brain compatibility, so must the transforming of schools into learning organizations be organized and administered in a brain-friendly manner.

THE CREATION OF LEARNING ORGANIZATIONS— BRAIN-COMPATIBLE STRATEGIES

One of the most critical aspects of brain research on learning is that elements of brain research are true not only for students but for ourselves as educators. In that regard, educators also do not learn without purpose and meaning or in high-threat environments. Viewing this from a different perspective, the creation of brain-based learning organizations can be looked upon as a response to a set of questions formulated by Wheatley (1993):

- What are the sources of order?
- How do we create organizational coherence where activities correspond to purpose?
- How do we create structures that move with change, that are flexible and adaptive, and that enable rather than constrain?

- How do we balance personal needs for freedom and autonomy with organizational needs for prediction and control?

To effectively respond to such questions we must first change the mental models about how schools are organized and how school decisions are made. The change in mental models is both complex and perceptual in nature. Thus, efforts to change mental models cannot be imposed, fragmented, or implemented in a mechanistic way.

Watkins and Marsick (1993) identify the attributes of a learning organization, emphasizing that no single formula for creating such an environment exists. They do, however, outline the following features that characterize learning organizations:

- Leaders who model calculated risk taking and experimentation
- Decentralized decision making and employee empowerment
- Skill inventories and audits of learning capacity
- Systems for sharing learning and using it within the organization
- Rewards and structures for employee initiatives
- Consideration of long-term consequences and impact on the work of others
- Frequent use of cross-functional work teams
- Opportunities to learn from experience on a daily basis
- A culture of feedback and disclosure

Germinario and Cram (1998) describe the characteristics of a learning organization within an educational context. These elements of the framework of a quality school include:

- The connection, supported by research, that instruction is most effective in a school environment characterized by norms of collegiality and continuous improvement
- The belief that teachers are professionals who should be given responsibility for the instructional process and held accountable for its outcomes
- The use of a wide range of practices and structures that enable administrators and teachers to work together on school improvement

- The involvement of teachers in decisions about school goals and the means for achieving them

If schools are to transform into learning organizations, administrators and teachers must change their respective mental models of how schools have traditionally operated. For this to be successful, three brain-compatible elements must be simultaneously at work: *relaxed alertness, orchestrated immersion,* and *active processing.*

RELAXED ALERTNESS

Threat and stress have a profound impact on how we create meaning and, ultimately, how we learn and behave. People respond to stress and threats differently. Some dismiss them, while others may consider them a challenge and rise to the occasion. Others find they cannot handle the stress, which, at times, can be almost debilitating, prompting a wide range of destructive behaviors. However, the brain responds to threats in predictable ways. The moment a threat is detected, the brain jumps into high gear. Immediately, chemical reactions within the brain change the way we think, feel, and act (Jensen, 1998).

Unfortunately, threat is one of the most common "motivating" strategies in schools. Teachers threaten students with poor grades, referrals to the principal's office, humiliation in front of other students, and calls to parents. Principals threaten teachers with poor performance ratings, transfers to undesirable positions, and, ultimately, loss of job. Superintendents threaten principals with poor performance ratings, loss of pay, and the economic and personal anguish of losing a job. Finally, school boards threaten the superintendent.

Within an organizational context, a climate that is characterized by high levels of stress will most likely prohibit a chance to create an organic environment for individual and/or school improvement. Because these emotions create a mental image of school life, teachers evolve into an unmotivated state. Jensen (1998) calls this phenomenon *learned helplessness.* He goes on to describe conditions that promote a state of learned helplessness:

Trauma: when an individual is engaged in a circumstance involving an important, uncontrollable event

Lack of control: when an individual either has no control over or lacks entirely the skills to effect his/her environment.

Decision: when an individual makes a paralyzing decision to explain an event or circumstance, such as "I'm to blame," "I can't do anything about it," or "I must not be able to do anything right."

Clearly, learning cannot flourish in a threatening and stressful climate. If learning is to occur, teachers must feel safe to experience new thoughts and experiment with new strategies. Typically, when threatened or in a stressful climate, teachers will devote most of their energy to defending how they feel, how they are thinking, or why they are behaving in a certain manner. It is inevitable that their ability to learn and their ability to be part of a learning community will be stifled. This, in turn, will most likely force the teachers to maintain established patterns of behaviors that feel safe even if they are not effective.

It is not easy to create a learning environment where external obstacles such as threats, challenges, and tension exist. Yet a concerted effort and commitment must be made by both administration and faculty to individually and collectively transform the way schools currently operate. The first step in this transformation is to recognize, as we believe to be true in student learning, that *emotions* are critical to learning and growth in adults. Emotions affect how a teacher feels about the climate in the school, which will, in time, create a personal meaning that is attached to the school environment. Positive emotions help guarantee that adults (as well as students) pay attention to the goals and focus of what is to be learned. Teachers will then interact within the school environment to learn more, to challenge their old assumptions, and to discard ideas that no longer make sense. This kind of learning captures a person's imagination and heart; this type of learning transforms a learner (Combs, Miser, and Whitaker, 1999). In short, the emotional element in creating a mental model is the critical interplay between how we feel, think, and act. Clearly, there is no separation of emotions, thinking, and learning.

Another critical element is the creation of a sense of *belonging* and *collegiality* with the school. This can be developed by planned activities that address the culture of isolation that often characterizes a teacher's life within the school. Little (1982) identified several types of such teacher interactions that define collegiality. They include teachers observing one another's teaching and providing meaningful feedback, and teachers jointly developing and sharing materials. Little asserts that these interactions engender a shared focus and language about teaching and promote meaningful discussions about school life.

Just as important is the need for school staff to *model brain-compatible learning behaviors*. We have long known the importance of being a role model for our students. In turn, the professional within the school must understand the significance of emotions when dealing with his/her colleagues. This is particularly true for school and district administrators. Much has been written about the school principal as the critical element in school improvement and reform initiatives. It, therefore, becomes a primary mission of the school principal to establish a school culture that values and encourages collegiality and collaboration. Special care must be given to consciously engage in planning for both formal and informal mechanisms to ensure teacher physical and emotional well-being.

Often the establishment of *rituals* and *celebrations* enhance a sense of belonging, collegiality, and safety. Recognition at a faculty meeting of a staff member's accomplishments, the development of a school motto or song, dress-up (or -down) days, luncheons, and so on, can help reduce organizational stress, as well as provide an emotional attachment to the goals of the school.

The evaluation process in schools is by nature a threatening experience that creates a conceptual divide between the evaluator (administrator) and the teacher. While the need for accountability in teacher performance is, and will likely always be, an important element of school improvement, consideration must be given to brain-based and adult learning characteristics. As with teacher professional development experiences, teacher accountability will be most successful within a context of *differentiated supervision*. A differentiated model bases supervisory practice on the developmental needs of the individual teacher. Such a model should move from direct supervisory intervention, assistance, and monitoring toward increasingly nondirective applications emphasizing self-initiated growth through reflection and problem solving.

The implementation of a differentiated supervisory model promotes a brain-compatible environment. Specifically, what is experienced by the teacher has personal meaning, it has the capability of challenging without the excessive threat of failure, and it engages teachers as active participants within the supervisory process.

ORCHESTRATED IMMERSION

A recurring theme within the context of brain-compatible learning is that we learn best when immersed in meaningful, compelling experiences. Yet all too often, teachers, in many schools, are looked upon as hierarchical subordinates who are not permitted access into the operation of the very schools in which they work. Thus, the mental model of school life for the typical teacher is developed around the emotions, patterns, and meanings that have influenced his/her *personal vision* of school life as it exists in the classroom. While these personal visions provide meaning to what teachers do within their respective classroom, they are unique to each teacher and do little to foster the goals of the entire (system) school.

The first step, then, to create opportunities for collaboration around meaningful activities is the development of a *shared vision*. Just as personal visions are pictures or images people carry in their heads, shared visions are pictures that people throughout the organization carry (Senge, 1990). When people truly share a vision, they are connected, bound together by a common aspiration (Senge, 1990, p. 206).

Creating a culture where the group collectively defines a picture of the future is quite complex. Yet the most fundamental aspect of this process must be based on the premise that the shared vision should be built upon the sum of the personal visions of all individuals within the school. Clearly, a shared vision cannot be imposed. Moreover, a shared vision cannot be in direct conflict with individual personal visions. The emergence of a shared vision can then only be fostered through meaningful collaboration among teachers and other major stakeholders within the school.

There is overwhelming evidence that the nature of the relationships among the adults who live and work in a school community has a tremendous influence upon the school's climate, its effectiveness, and the level of student performance (Smith and Scott, 1990). Thus, it is essential in the creation of a brain-compatible organizational culture that special care be given to opportunities for collaboration and shared governance.

The importance of collaboration in the development of a positive school culture is not new. Teachers are often asked to serve on ad hoc problem-solving committees, are encouraged to share teaching materials, and, at times, to collaborate on teaching units or lessons. While valuable, these periodic, limited experiences do little to promote a culture of collaboration that systematically involves teachers in the organization and development of the entire school (system). Involved in such a culture, teachers can experience a sense of wholeness, or what Crowell (1998) calls a "dynamic unity," that is, opportunities where teachers can extract meaningful patterns and school-wide relationships.

From a practical perspective the reasons for collaboration are self-evident. First, problems are best resolved by those closely associated with the problem, and the implementation of the solution to the problem is more effectively carried out when those responsible for the implementation have ownership in the solution. Second, the nature and complexity of the challenges facing most schools can no longer simply be met by individuals within the school working independent of other professionals and resources (Germinario and Cram, 1998). Additionally, meaningful immersion of teachers in collaboration activities can serve as a model for what we hope all students will learn. Richardson, Lane, and Jackson (1995) provide the following perspective: "If we want students who will learn to make decisions, to work with others and to solve problems, then teachers must be heavily involved in making the decisions that affect their work and the life of the school" (p. 117).

From a brain-based perspective, opportunities for teachers to be immersed as part of the whole system (school) helps provide a greater sense of wholeness and deeper meaning of how their personal vision interacts with the school's shared vision. By doing so, patterns are developed that tie together isolated experiences and pieces of information, giving cohesive meaning and purpose to daily school life. Additionally, the human brain is a social brain (Gazzaniga, 1985). It is clear that we have a brain-based drive to belong to a group and relate to others. Thus, collaboration with colleagues satisfies a neurological predisposition that contributes to security and relaxed alertness as well as the brain's need to search for patterns and connections.

Both immersion and collaboration are management processes borrowed from what has been learned about effective business practices. Within a school organization, Richardson, Lane, and Jackson (1995) describe it as "a process or philosophy to improve educational outcomes by increasing the autonomy of those operating within the educational system to make decisions and share the responsibility for those decisions with everyone who has an interest in the educational process" (p. 119). The most common means to promote this opportunity occurs through site-based management teams.

According to the American Association of School Administrators (AASA), the National Association of Elementary School Administrators (NAESP), and the National Association of Secondary School Principals (NASSP), school-based planning teams:

- Allow competent individuals in the school to make decisions that affect them with the focus on improving learning
- Give the entire school community a voice in key decisions
- Focus accountability for decisions, leading to a greater creativity in the design of programs and redirection of resources to support the goals developed in the school
- Lead to realistic budgeting as teachers and parents become more aware of the school's financial status, spending limitations, and the cost of its programs
- Improve morale of teachers and nurture new leadership at all levels of the school organization

Unlike the *myth of the management team* discussed earlier (p. 143), where an ad hoc team is created to address specific problems, a site-based management team representing consistent commitment to the involvement of professionals in the decision-making process can yield positive results. When effectively implemented, site-based management teams can enhance the professionals in the school as a *learning organization,* one "where people continually expand their capacity to create the results they truly desire, where new and expansive patterns of thinking are nurtured, where collective aspiration is set free, and where people are continually learning how to learn together" (Senge, 1990, p. 3).

ACTIVE PROCESSING

Orchestrated immersion and relaxed alertness are of critical importance in the brain's ongoing search for meaning. Yet, to maximize connections, gain deeper insights, and perceive additional possibilities that may be hidden in experience, the brain must consciously work for them. Caine and Caine (1991) call this aspect of brain-based learning *active processing*. They describe the concept as the consolidation and internalization of information, by the learner, in a way that is both personally meaningful and conceptually coherent. It is a path to understanding rather than simply to memory (p. 147).

Thus, from an organizational perspective, it is simply not enough to provide a safe environment that promotes collaboration and shared meaning. Schools must actively seek ways for teachers to process what they have learned and decided upon. In developing this new paradigm, traditional beliefs and hierarchical relations must be challenged. This is by no means an easy task. For decades the structure of schools has done little to allow and encourage teachers to seek new roles in influencing and reshaping educational practices. Interestingly, teachers are held accountable for a system that they have had little opportunity to help design. It is no wonder, then, that teachers are reluctant to change, take risks, or challenge the status quo.

For teachers to become meaningful participants in the school as a learning organization, we must enrich their roles in the leadership of the school. *Teachers as leaders* has become a common theme within the school-restructuring literature. Much has been written concerning the positive individual and school outcomes associated with the empowering of teachers, giving them meaningful ways to influence and act upon decisions that affect their working environment.

Pounder and Ogawa (1995), studying leadership as an organizational quality, suggest that the total amount of leadership found in schools will have a positive relationship to their performance. Further, they suggest that all members of the school, including the teachers, can lead and thus affect the performance of their school. Teacher leaders (like other school leaders) affect school performance by shaping the organization of work, developing solidarity among organizational members, managing the schools' relation with their external environments, and building members' commitment to their schools. The basic premise for empowering teachers to assume leadership roles is the belief that those closest to existing problems have the expertise to solve them. Howey (1988, p. 29) provides additional support for teacher leadership as based on the need for "highly competent leaders who reside where the problems primarily are—in schools—and who can address these in a continuing collective manner."

Engaging teachers as leaders in actively processing the shared goals and initiatives of the school is exceedingly important in promoting a brain-friendly environment. In a very real sense it helps them make sense of their experiences. Caine and Caine (1991) suggest that the pervasive objective is to focus on the process of our learning and extract and articulate what has been explored and what it means. In effect, the teacher asks, "What did I do?" "Why did I do it?" and "What did I learn?"

While immersing teachers in leadership roles within the school is not a common phenomenon, Henderson (1995) has identified and described six leadership roles that teachers can actively participate in:

1. *Master teacher*. The assumption is that teaching expertise provides a foundation for other leadership roles. The skills inherent in a master teacher are essential to assisting inexperienced and/or less effective teachers. Similarly, the master teacher's success in designing and implementing effective teaching/learning strategies can initiate professional growth activities leading to other leadership roles.
2. *Curriculum specialist*. The knowledge base developed through interest and experience in specific curricular areas makes the teacher a valuable resource in designing and evaluating curriculum.
3. *Mentor*. The significance of internships and induction processes place additional importance on the teacher's leadership role in the professional development of novice teachers.
4. *Teacher educator*. A traditional role of teachers has been providing leadership in the ongoing professional development of other teachers. This role has focused on serving as a model in demonstrating skills and dispositions.
5. *Student advocate*. The teacher has the most contact and interaction

with students. Information about student achievement, attendance, needs, home life, and so on, come from teachers. To that end, teachers have the most significant role in developing leadership skills that address issues related to improving instruction, curriculum, and school climate for the benefit of students.

6. *Researcher.* This role provides an important way to link theory and practice, to look anew at everyday activities, and to inform about the classroom ways children learn and teachers teach.

To develop a deeper meaning of school life for teachers, the challenge exists to develop teachers into leadership roles. Clearly, concepts related to culture and leadership opportunity are both interactive and cyclical. That is, while culture influences risk taking and willingness to change, establishing ways for teachers to assume meaningful leadership roles influences school culture. These opportunities for teacher leaders are possible on a broad continuum from informal to formal, with an impact on both individual and school-wide practices.

ADMINISTRATIVE LEADERSHIP: MOVING OUT OF THE COMFORT ZONE

While somewhat difficult to describe, leadership has and will be a critical ingredient for school improvement. Traditionally, leadership in schools has been vested in the principal, who by the nature of his/her position is charged with managing the daily activities in the building. This prevailing view has often led to vast differences in the way schools are organized, run, and maintained. These differences reflect the principal's values and beliefs and the degree to which teachers choose to adhere to the principal's directions.

The roots of this traditional perspective can be traced to the beginning of the twentieth century and find their foundation in management and the utilization of formal authority and power. Over the past twenty-five years a wide variety of leadership theories and approaches have found their way into schools. These include management by objectives, Theory Z, value chain analysis, quality circles, restructuring, management by walking around, and the one-minute management. While by no means an exhaustive list of innovations, they give some "flavor" of the constant search for effective ways to lead.

Most all leadership concepts begin in organizations outside of schools. Although we do not definitively know how these concepts apply in a school setting, school leaders continue to search for tools, such as those just mentioned, to foster effective schools. Evans (1996) describes the life cycle of leadership theory in education:

1. It begins outside of education, developed by political scientists from studies of gifted historical figures or by management experts from studies of gifted business leaders.
2. It gains favor in corporate America and comes to be a hot concept in management writing.
3. As it nears the apex of its influence, someone decides to apply it to education, even if it has little apparent relevance to schools.
4. It grows hot in educational circles as it begins to cool in the corporate world, where it is showing hitherto unnoticed weaknesses.
5. It is often misapplied in education either through slavish rigidity (failing to modify the model to fit schools' unique characteristics) or false clarity (adopting the form of the innovation but not its true substance).
6. Well after it has lost its cachet among business leaders, it lingers on in vestigial form in schools and schools of education, until its popularity finally subsides there too (pp. 146–147).

Fortunately, the thinking on leadership in schools has changed, in that it has transcended simple notions of management and power. After decades of emphasis on science, techniques, models, and style, leadership theory has centered on the notion of *transformation*. The most important task of the transformational leader is to establish a school culture that values and encourages leadership at all levels of school organization. Whether through formal collaborative teams, consensus building, modeling, or personal influence, the principal must promote a school's vision for success by establishing a culture where staff, students, and community members have school goals that become more important than their own self-interests. In this new role of *cultural leader,* the principal seeks to define, strengthen, and articulate enduring values and beliefs that give the school its unique identity and purpose.

This change in the leadership role of the principal has prompted a major shift among those who study leadership and among those who practice it. Despite different styles, principals in successful schools have a transformational effect on the people who work in the shadow of their leadership. As Roberts (1985) explains, the collective action that transforms leadership generally empowers those who participate in the process. There is hope, there is optimism, there is energy. In essence, transforming leadership is a leadership that facilitates the redefinition of a people's mission and vision, a renewal of their commitment, and the restructuring of their systems for goal accomplishment (p. 1024).

Leithwood (1992) describes transformational leadership as a form of consensual or facilitative power that is manifested through other people instead of over other people. The "old" way of leadership is hierarchical and authoritarian; the "new" way seeks to gain the overall participation of others.

Walker (March, 1993) defines three kinds of transformational leadership approaches:

1. *A collaborative, shared decision-making approach:* Such leaders believe that organizational goals can be better accomplished by shared commitment and collaboration.
2. *An emphasis on teacher professionalism and teacher empowerment:* Such leaders believe all teachers are capable of leadership and encourage them to be self-directed.
3. *An understanding of change, including how to encourage change in others:* Such leaders are agents of change and are committed to educating students for the twenty-first century.

Sagar (1992) reports that an increasing trend in schools where teachers and students report a culture conducive to school success is that a transformational leader is the principal. He goes on to suggest that these principals consistently utilize identifiable strategies:

- A clear and unified focus that empowers professionals to act as both individuals and members of the school
- A common cultural perspective that enables teachers to view other schools through a similar lens
- A constant push for improvement emphasizing the importance of

the simultaneous application of pressure and support during educational change

Developing a culture that fosters a transformation from power vested
in an individual to power vested among stakeholders is both complex
and challenging. To initiate this change, principals (and those in other
traditional school leadership positions) must foster the notion of schools
as learning organizations. To that end, Watkins and Marsick (1996) provide a set of key initiatives that learning communities must follow:

- Create continuous learning opportunities.
- Promote inquiry and dialogue.
- Encourage collaboration and team learning.
- Create systems to capture and share learning.
- Empower people toward a collective vision.
- Connect the organization (school) to its greater environment.
- Provide strategic leadership for learning.

In a very real way the transformation of the school's leader into one
who promotes a culture of continuous learning finds its foundation in
brain-based research. Most importantly, school administrators must first
realize that they can either enhance or inhibit the natural operation of the
brain's search for meaning. This search can only be fostered in a safe,
secure environment that genuinely involves teachers in all aspects of
school life and school improvement efforts. To do so the school administrator will be able to utilize what we know about brain-based learning
to create a learning organization with a focus on problem solving and
improvement. To that end, the following concepts should become the
foundation from which the school administrator approaches this transformation:

1. The brain is a learning organ that rarely rests and is constantly
   searching for meaning. The actions of the administrator continue to
   provide the basis for the mental model teachers develop about their
   role in the school.
2. The *brain is a dynamic processor of information*. Teachers' under-

standing of how classrooms and schools work is a critical variable in any effort to solve school problems and/or improve school life.

3. *Learning is a sociocognitive act bringing social interaction and cognitive processing together in an interactive manner.* Administrators must provide opportunities to use teachers in problem-solving groups, as mentors, and on school governance councils.

4. *Multisensory activities that embed skills in natural experiences tend to enhance the brain's search for meaning.* Administrators must promote opportunities for teachers to engage in activities (such as action research) that help them construct their own perspective on how best to operate their classrooms.

5. *To learn, the brain requires one to act on the learning.* To this end, teachers must be given the opportunity to actively process the vision that they have helped create for the school.

Managing and leading within the school environment has become increasingly more complex. Yet what we now know about the brain and how it can facilitate student learning can ultimately help in the administration of our schools. This can happen when administrators model an understanding of brain-based research and model a passion for the creation of a learning organization (school), just as teachers foster a learning organization in their classrooms.

SUMMARY

This chapter examined the dynamics of school organization and leadership. Specifically, characteristics associated with the development of learning organizations were provided. Additionally, specific strategies associated with brain-based research were provided as a way to enhance organizational and school effectiveness.

Finally, consistent with the recurring theme of this book, the assumption is made that when the adults in the school understand and work within a brain-friendly environment, it becomes more likely that their classrooms and teaching strategies will reflect the benefits of brain-based research.

REFERENCES

Argyris, Chris. (1990). *Overcoming Organizational Deficiencies*. New York: Prentice Hall.

Caine, Renate N. and Geoffrey Caine. (1991). *Making Connections: Teaching and the Human Brain*. Alexandria, VA: Association of Supervision and Curriculum Development.

Combs, Arthur W., Ann B. Miser, and Kathryn S. Whitaker. (1999). *On Becoming a School Leader*. Alexandria, VA: Association of Supervision and Curriculum Development.

Crowell, S. (1998). "A New Way of Thinking: The Challenge of the Future." *Educational Leadership,* 47 (1), 60.

Evans, Robert. (1996). *The Human Side of School Change*. San Francisco: Jossey-Bass.

Gazzaniga, M. (1985). *The Social Brain: Discovering the Networks of the Mind*. New York: Basic Books.

Germinario, Vito and Henry G. Cram. (1998). *Change for Public Education: Practical Approaches for the 21st Century*. Lancaster, PA: Technomic Publishing Company.

Glickman, Carl D. (1992). "The Essence of School Renewal: The Prose Has Begun." *Educational Leadership,* 50 (1), 24–27.

Henderson-Sparks, Joan C. (1995). "Managing Your Marginal Teachers." *Principal,* 74 (4), 32–35.

Howey, K. (1988). "Why Teach Leadership?" *Journal of Teacher Education,* 39 (1), 28–30.

Jensen, Eric. (1998). *Teaching with the Brain in Mind*. Alexandria, VA: Association for Supervision and Curriculum Development.

Leithwood, Kenneth. (1992). "The Move Toward Transformational Leadership." *Educational Leadership,* 49 (5), 34–35.

Little, Judith W. (1982). "Norms of Collegiality and Experimentation: Workplace Conditions of School Success." *American Research Journal,* 3, 325–340.

Ogden, Evelyn H. and Vito Germinario. (1995). *The Nation's Best Schools: Blueprints for Excellence. Volume 2, Middle and Secondary School*. Lancaster, PA: Technomic Publishing Company.

Pounder, Diana G. and Rodney T. Ogawa. (1995). "Leadership as an Organization-wide Phenomenon: Its Impact on School Performance." *Educational Administrative Quarterly,* 31 (4), 564–588.

Richardson, Michael D., Kenneth E. Lane, and L. Jackson. (1995). *School Empowerment*. Lancaster, PA: Technomic Publishing Company.

Roberts, N. (1985). "Transforming Leaders: A Process of Collective Action." *Human Relations,* 38 (11), 1023–1046.

Sagar, Richard D. (1992). "Three Principals Who Make a Difference." *Educational Leadership,* 49 (5), 13–18.

Senge, Peter M. (1990). *The Fifth Discipline.* New York: Doubleday.

Smith, Stuart C. and James J. Scott. (1990). *A Work Environment for Effective Instruction.* Alexandria, VA: National Association of Secondary Principals.

Walker, Bradford L. (March, 1993). "What It Takes to Be an Empowering Principal." *Principal* (77) 552, 41–42.

Watkins, Karen E. and Victoria J. Marsick. (1990). *In Action: Creating the Learning Organization,* Volume I. Alexandria, VA: American Society for Training and Development.

———. (1993). *Sculpting the Learning Organization: Lesson in the Art of Systemic Change.* San Francisco: Jossey-Bass.

———. (1996). "Adult Educators and the Challenge of the Learning Organization." *Adult Learning,* 7 (4), 18–20.

Wheatley, M. J. (1993). *Leadership and the New Science.* San Francisco: Berrett-Koehler.

CHAPTER 8

The Learning Community—
How It All Adds Up

> In a learning community the goal is to advance the collective knowledge and, in that way, support the growth of individual knowledge.
>
> M. Scardamalia and C. Berester

The dominant value and belief systems of a school determine the observable characteristics and the essence of the school as an organization, a place. These underlying values and beliefs define "what we do in this school," "how we make decisions," "how we respond to parents and the community," "what the real operating objectives are that we act upon," "what we perceive as our accountability for what students learn," "what we consider important for students to learn," "how we interact with our colleagues," "what we believe about what students can learn," "why the staff works here," and "what we perceive as valued by the board of education, the central office, parents, and community." No school or district is purely one type; however, how the school leadership and staff, how district leadership and staff, how boards of education, and how community members act on the answers to these questions creates the culture, the climate, the character, and, ultimately, the degree of effectiveness of the school and school district.

Glickman (1993) provides a characterization of schools in terms of their basic beliefs and values. Further, he describes them as being either *conventional, congenial,* or *collegial.*

165

THE CONVENTIONAL SCHOOL

In the "conventional" school, classrooms function largely as autonomous units: the school is a loose collection of these separate classrooms. These are schools that have no common goals, no collective sense of what they are trying to accomplish. Each classroom is like a minischool. Teachers work in isolation within their own rooms. Although people usually work very hard, they view their work as what they do in their own classroom or maybe at their own grade level. What happens in the individual classroom depends on the beliefs, values, knowledge, and experiences of the individual teacher. Most of the staff believe that everyone else in the school shares the same beliefs about teaching and learning that they do; however, this is rarely the case.

The principal views his/her role primarily as that of a manager, that is, someone who makes sure that the school runs well, teachers have the materials they need, discipline is maintained, parental concerns are handled, and the PTA receives assistance for projects they undertake. Rules and sets of operational procedures often give the impression of strong building-level leadership and control; however, what are controlled are the operational aspects of the school. The principal's beliefs, often shared by district administration, form the basis of how he/she interprets his/her role, what he/she values, and the basic climate and culture of the school.

Conventional school "leadership" is defined in terms of efficient operational management and public relations. Stability, lack of conflict, and minimal intervention or upset in terms of the instructional process will be valued. Broad-based instructional planning, for example, would conflict with the value placed on individual teacher autonomy and stability and, therefore, is not characteristic of these schools. Even where there is site-based management, planning is usually confined to such areas as development of a new disciplinary policy, bus loading and unloading procedures, or student scheduling. Planning for change in instructional practice is considered inconsistent with the belief that this area is the prerogative of the individual teacher. Since the concept of staff development is inconsistent with conventional school beliefs concerning the importance or, in fact, the ability of teachers to make major changes in practice, little value is placed on staff development and teacher evaluation. Inservice opportunities are usually limited to specific days in the district calendar and provide a smorgasbord of activities designed to allow for maximum options for individual teachers to make decisions about what to attend. Staff meetings are kept to a minimum and focus mainly on procedures and events involving the entire school, i.e., schedules for "back-to-school" night. Teacher evaluation is considered a bureaucratic requirement; at best, the formal evaluation process provides the opportunity to support, in writing, what teachers are doing and a means for weeding out weak, nontenured teachers; at worst, the formal evaluation process is viewed by the principal and teachers as an unwelcome and unnecessary interference in the individual classroom and a waste of valuable time.

THE CONGENIAL SCHOOL

The "congenial" school gives the impression of being a cohesive unit with common goals. There are a lot of meetings and a lot of communication. The employees have a strong sense of being a school; it is a nice place to work. However, close inspection of the operational goals and priorities reveals that the focus is on the adults: improving the climate for adults, improving communication among teachers, and relieving teacher stress (Glickman, 1993). The belief is that the school should also be a nice place for students—friendly, supportive, concerned with self-esteem—and that there should be a friendly relationship between staff and parents. In other words, the "happy" school is the "good" school. However, when you get past the focus on affect, particularly for the adults, there is little difference between the congenial school and the conventional school in terms of beliefs about how children should learn, how instruction should be delivered, and how learning should be assessed.

As in the conventional school, the principal's role is defined mostly in operational and management terms. His/her role is to provide support for individual teachers in terms of classroom material, discipline, and support with parents; however, greater emphasis is placed on pleasing and being liked by parents and teachers. The value placed on public relations leads to actions that minimize the potential for conflict, to an even greater extent than in the conventional school. Value is placed on getting along by going along with the school as a clean, safe, and fun place to be. Change is viewed as having the potential of "rocking the boat." Since common goals concerning the instructional outcomes of education are missing, classroom practices reflect beliefs concerning the autonomy of teachers within the classroom; the idea that learning is limited, based on what the child brings to school; lack of relevance of knowledge and practice outside the school; and satisfaction with the status quo. The emphasis on affect frequently leads to lower standards for at least some children, justified by the belief that, if children are challenged, they may experience failure and low self-esteem. A reward for staff for working in the congenial school comes from the "family-type" atmosphere throughout the school. However, the reward for students in terms of learning may be no greater than in the conventional school.

THE COLLEGIAL SCHOOL

The third type of school, frequently referred to as the "collegial" school, operates from a very different belief system concerning the nature and purposes of the school. Staff derive satisfaction from professional work accomplished together and from the achievement of children. These schools are bound by a strong sense of common mission and goals for student learning outcomes. Characteristic of the leadership and staff is that they are never satisfied, that it can always be better. They believe the following:

1. Instructional leadership
   - The purpose of the school is student learning; all children can learn to a very high set of standards.
   - The most important roles of the principal are to make explicit the belief and value systems of the school, exhibit behaviors that reflect the beliefs of the school, lead the continuing effort toward improvement, foster staff development, find time for planning and analysis, and communicate the mission and outcomes to parents, the community, and the central office.

- The principal is the leader of the school instructional team, emphasizing that "we know more together about effective practice than any one person alone."

2. Management
   - Ensuring a safe and orderly school environment is an important function of the principal. In order to operate efficiently, the school needs sets of common procedures and practices, such as disciplinary policies and procedures, schedules, written curriculum and textbooks for each grade level, standard report card and parent conference procedures, and means for reporting assessment results to parents.

3. Instructional accountability
   - The staff of the school is accountable for the learning of students — if we only work hard enough and are smart enough and creative enough, then every last child will achieve mastery in every content area.
   - Standards for student achievement proposed by professional associations, national committees, and states are valuable for determining what children should learn.

4. Research on instruction and learning
   - As a profession, educators know a great deal about how students learn and how they should be taught; their findings are applicable to what happens in their school.
   - Teachers and principals continue to learn, to get better at what they do.
   - Colleagues have valuable lessons to share; working together will improve education for children.

5. School improvement and planning
   - Education is never totally fixed, and major school stakeholders should not wait until it breaks to work at improving it; data concerning the outcomes and processes of education should continually be probed to identify areas of need; it is okay to share flaws with staff, parents, and the community, since they can be trusted to know that the school is working on continual improvement.
   - The change process takes time—time to study data, time to ask fundamental questions, time to research solutions, time to make connections among programs and practices, time to plan, time to

train staff, time to implement, and time to reassess. Participating in these activities is a vital part of being in the education profession.

- The staff needs to share a common vocabulary and set of common definitions so that they can communicate effectively among themselves, with students, and with parents.
- Change brings an expected degree of anxiety and stress; however, change is essential. Not everyone will be totally happy with everyone else's position on every issue, not everyone will agree on certain means or even the value of certain ends, but that is the price everyone is willing to pay on the road to creating a more effective school.
- Carefully thought-out risk taking is encouraged—it is okay to "play" with new ideas.
- Outside agencies, universities, businesses, parents, and other schools can help in the quest.
- The highest form of satisfaction, as a professional, comes from the intrinsic knowledge that you have made a difference—been part of something beyond personal goals.

These underlying beliefs create the climate of the student outcome based school and determine what is valued, what is reinforced, what is done, and what the outcomes are. It follows, then, that in these schools, "leadership" is defined largely in terms of instruction. Therefore, the principal needs to know a lot about how children learn, about instructional practice and curriculum, and how he/she can assess outcome data, monitor instruction, study the research, and network with instructional leaders outside of the school. Teachers believe in the benefits of the collegial process of instructional improvement. It follows, then, that they must be actively involved in ongoing learning and staff development, as well as being participants in planning. As a result, staff development is a high priority in collegial schools. Since staff act on the belief that every student will learn, data concerning the outcomes of learning are disaggregated and studied. Since standards for learning are valued, the staff is concerned with setting standards and, therefore, is willing to look outside proposed standards for instruction and learning.

While no school will exactly match the prototypes just presented, such a characterization does provide a framework to assess one's school on an identified continuum. If one believes (as these authors do) that the elements embodied in the "collegial schools" have the most potential to best serve students, then one quickly identifies that potential is focused on a continuing process of learning and improving. This perspective has, until recently, relied upon behavioral sciences and successful practice as the basis for school improvement. Yet, to truly evolve into organic learning organizations, schools must integrate the significant contributions in the cognitive sciences and neurobiology that provide great insight into how both the students and the adults within the school learn. The successful application and integration of this knowledge will transform schools into *communities of learners.*

TOWARD A COMMUNITY OF LEARNERS

Moving a school from one that emphasizes individuals to one that values organizational learning is quite complex. All stakeholders within the school community must be provided an opportunity to share, learn, and continually transform themselves as the organization transforms itself. Marquardt (1996) concludes that learning must take place almost as a by-product of people doing the work—in contrast to acquiring knowledge before performing a particular task or job (p. 17). This constructivist perspective provides the members of the school community an opportunity to create a collective meaning and deep understanding of life within the school. Further, the schools become places where all members of the school community can continually search for understanding, appreciate uncertainty, inquire systematically, and learn collectively.

Similarly, Watkins and Marsick (1999) identify three levels of interrelated learning:

- *Individual learning:* the way in which people make meaning of their experiences, and how the organization provides them with opportunities to build their knowledge and skills
- *Team learning:* the way in which groups of people work and learn collaboratively and, as a result, create new knowledge together as well as create the capacity for collaborative action
- *Organizational learning:* shared thinking and the capacity of a system that is embodied in procedures, artifacts and mental models

BRAIN-BASED COMMUNITIES OF LEARNERS

The principles addressed in this book have provided the foundation for the integration of the cognitive sciences into school life. These principles, if understood and utilized, can be a powerful tool in the transformation of schools into continual-learning organizations.

Most schools value and provide opportunities for staff development and training. These activities are usually aimed at enhancing professional skills to improve the quality of teaching in individual classrooms. While this effort is significant for each individual, little is done to create school conditions and processes that support continual learning, adaptation, or change. Conversely, learning communities recognize that it is no longer appropriate, or exceedingly useful, to study individual parts of the school organization and its members in isolation. In short, emphasis must be placed on the connections between the beliefs and actions of all stakeholders within the school community and the overall mission of the school.

Brandt (1998, p. 51) compares learning by individuals with learning by organizations:

Learning Individuals	Learning Organizations
Learn what is personally meaningful, what they feel a need to learn.	Have an incentive structure that encourages adaptive behavior.
Learn when they accept challenging goals, go through developmental stages.	Have challenging but achievable shared goals.
Learn in their own way.	Have members who can accurately identify the organization's stages of development.
Construct new knowledge by building on old.	Gather, process, and act upon information in ways best suited to their purposes.
Learn through social interaction.	Have an institutional knowledge base and processes for creating new ideas.
Need feedback.	Exchange information frequently with relevant external sources.

Develop and use strategies (Learn how to learn.)

Learn well in a positive emotional climate.

Learn from the total environment, intended and unintended.

Get feedback on products and services.

Continually refine their basic processes.

Have a supportive organizational culture.

Are "open systems" sensitive to the external environment, including social, political, and economic conditions.

Create Safe Environments for Continual-Learning Opportunities

Research strongly suggests that stress negatively affects decision making and judgment and impairs memory and learning. The body responds to negative stress by releasing moderate amounts of the hormone cortisol. High levels of cortisol induce despair and feelings of being overwhelmed and impair thinking.

Threats and unattainable challenges cause the brain to trigger a sense of fear or anxiety and a sense of helplessness. O'Keefe and Nadel (1978) have found that under any type of perceived threat, the brain:

- Loses its ability to take subtle clues from the environment
- Reverts to the familiar "tried-and-true" behaviors
- Loses some of its ability to index, store, and access information
- Loses some of its ability to perceive relationships and patterns
- Is less able to exercise "higher-order" thinking skills
- Loses some memory capacity
- Tends to overreact to stimuli—in almost a "phobic" way

As emphasized throughout this book, learning situations must be accompanied by a state of relaxed alertness, which creates a state of being that focuses the learner's attention on the task at hand. Thus, the first step in the creation of a community of learners is to assess and enrich the nature of the learning climate and culture.

The Brain Is a Social Brain, So Learning Is Fundamentally a Social Phenomenon

People organize their learning around the social communities to which they belong. Within the learning community, administrators, teachers, parents, students, and other community members engage in team learning experiences that encourage discussion, commitment, and purposeful reflection. Jensen (1995) describes this organizational structure as "sideways," that is, not bottom up or top down but participatory at all levels. The critical question, he concludes, is then "Do you share the knowledge you gain with others, consistently?" (p. 328). This emphasis on collaboration provides a distinct neurobiological benefit. Additionally, it typically provides for collective results that are greater than the sum of all individual efforts.

Thus, the second significant element in the creation of a community of learners is the creation of learning teams where members collaboratively construct new knowledge. Critical actions of this feature are focused on creating a culture in which people feel they are all part of the same team.

Empowerment—The Opportunity to Contribute Creates the Ongoing Potential for Learning

Circumstances in which members of the school engage in relevant activities that have consequences for both themselves and the learning community create a very powerful learning environment. In short, knowledge is inseparable from doing. The third critical element in the development of learning communities is the establishment of a culture where members are providing ongoing opportunities to identify and engage in real-life problem-solving activities. To that end, concepts related to the immersion in meaningful, compelling experiences is essential to empowerment. Further, members of the learning community must be given the time, responsibility, and resources to freely pursue what they believe to be relevant and important. Jensen (1995) concludes that the brain doesn't learn very well by forcing outcomes and is least effective when the learning is predisposed to rules, structures, and time limits. He goes on to indicate that learning is facilitated when five conditions are met:

- The environment is flooded with real-life experiences.
- The learners have a choice in what is to be learned as well as in how and when it is to be learned.
- The learning has ongoing feedback without formal monitoring systems that induce threat or anxiety.
- The learners are able to learn at their own pace.
- The learners' affective needs are accommodated so that they feel safe.

The brain has the ability to grow and adapt in response to environmental stimuli and life experiences. This plasticity encourages growth in synaptic connections and promotes real meaning and learning. Thus, if learning communities are to develop, it is essential that their members are empowered to engage in relevant, complex learning experiences.

Creation of a Shared Vision

Vision provides a clear statement of what the school looks like and delivers, as well as describes the environment in which it will operate. It includes the identification of an "ideal world" or the construction of the "best or preferred future" before injecting reality data (Kaufman and Herman, 1991).

Glickman (1992) speaks to a "supervision" for school success. He concludes that for a school to be educationally successful, it must be a community of professionals working toward a vision of teaching and learning that transcends individual classrooms, grade levels, and departments. The entire school community must develop a covenant to guide future decisions about the goals and operation of the school.

Lashway (1997) concludes that the vision of a school represents the unique values and beliefs of the people in a particular school and provides several generalizations concerning the kind of ideas that are typically found in vision of schools:

- *Visions are about what, and how, students will learn.* A focus on children is basic to any vision, says Lashway. Possible vision statements include: "Students will spend less time memorizing and more time solving problems" and "Content will be presented holistically and thematically, not chopped into subject-sized fragments."

- *Visions are about social justice.* Education must be committed to educating all children. Visions that encompass this idea might include: "Student opportunities for learning will be influenced more by students' interests and abilities than by class, race, or gender" and "Schools will develop a keen sense of social responsibility and a commitment to democratic processes."
- *Visions are about the kind of professional environment the school will provide.* Visions that address this issue include: "Students will become 'learning organizations,' providing intellectual stimulation and continual opportunities for professional development" and "Decisions will be made through dialogue and consensus rather than by bureaucratic mandates."
- *Visions are about the ways that schools will relate to the outside world.* Schools are sometimes isolated from the social mainstream. Visions that address this problem might be: "Educators and community members will find common ground through mutually respectful dialogue rather than political maneuvering" and "Schools will form external partnerships with businesses and community agencies."

Clearly, the most meaningful visions are those that are collaboratively developed through dialogue where the members of the organization share their mental images of what is embodied in a successful school. This picture of the future includes the deep-seated beliefs of each individual within the learning community. Thus, the shared vision becomes the sum of the personal visions of all participating individuals (Senge, 1990).

The real value of a shared vision is that it provides both the focus and the energy for ongoing shared learning. Additionally, it helps connect and bound together group members through a common goal.

Senge (1990, p. 223) concludes that building a shared vision is actually a piece of a larger activity: developing the "governing ideas" for the organization; its vision, purpose, or mission; and its core values. These governing ideas answer three critical questions: "What?" "Why?" and "How?"

- Vision is the "what"—the picture of the future that is being created.
- Purpose (mission) is the "why"—the organization's answer to the question "Why do we exist?"
- Core values answer the question "How do we want to act, consistent with our mission, along the path toward achieving our vision?" They describe how the organization wants life to be on a day-to-day basis while pursuing the vision.

The establishment of a shared vision focuses knowledge and learning on shared values, beliefs, and the ways of doing things. They include a multiplicity of points of view, yet eventually construct a clear mental image that serves to guide school planning, development, and evaluation.

Collaboration and Team Learning

Watkins and Marsick (1999) describe team learning as the mutual construction of new knowledge and the capacity for concerted, collaborative action. In schools, these types of activities take place all the time. Yet, often, members of the school community limit their full collaboration based on their established mental models of hierarchical structures. Traditional views of individual roles and notions of "who's in charge" often keep group members from functioning as equal partners in learning.

Similarly, creating participatory collaborative structures, such as site-based management teams and peer coaching, may produce what Evans (1996) has called "contrived collegiality." While having some value, such structures may not, by themselves, change the underlying norms, values, and mental models that produce meaningful collaboration and team learning. The real challenge lies in the ability of the group to alter its preconceived assumptions about collaboration and think freely toward collective problem solving. A key element of this challenge is the quality of dialogue among group members to create a collective meaning around school issues and improvement efforts.

Senge (1990, pp. 236–237) describes three critical dimensions of collaboration and team learning. First, there is a need to think insightfully about complex issues. This occurs when the collective potential for team problem solving becomes greater than that of the individuals in the group.

Second, there is a need for innovative, coordinated action. Here the team develops an "operational trust," where each team member remains conscious of other team members and can be counted on to act in ways that complement one another's actions.

Third, there is a role for the members of other teams. That is, learning teams have systemic linkages to other learning teams. This interactive phenomenon provides a way to integrate the skills of team learning across an organization.

The sharing of knowledge and experiences among members of a team is an essential element of brain-based learning. Learning is shaped by both internal processes and social interaction. Team learning permits group members to construct a collective meaning of school life. Through this an optimal learning situation is developed where learning is promoted through the active processing of hands-on experiences as well as dialogue with others. Our brains have a baseline of neural connectivity, and enriching activities such as those embodied in creative problem solving adds to that baseline. The critical ingredient to enriching the potential for team learning exists in the opportunity for members to be challenged with new information and/or experiences. There must be a mechanism to learn from the experience through interactive feedback. Meaningful collaboration and team learning experiences provide a foundation for both of these ingredients.

Systems Thinking—Understanding the Big Picture

The final element of developing a community of learners is group members recognizing the patterns that connect what they are doing to the larger system. Senge (1990, p. 68) describes systems thinking as a discipline for seeking wholes. It is a framework for identifying interrelationships rather than things, for seeing patterns rather than static snapshots. Caine and Caine (1991) emphasized the function of the neocortex as both a pattern maker and a pattern detector. This provides the ability to make sense of isolated pieces of information and is critical to understanding and motivation. Since the brain's craving for meaning is automatic, patterning occurs all the time. Each pattern that is discovered is added to the learner's "perceptual map," therefore leading to a more power mental model.

As organization members develop a perceptual map of the relation-ships between what they do and the mission of the school, they become sensitized to how they fit within the "big picture." A knowledge and appreciation for the big picture helps teachers to understand how their individual work adds to the collective work of the organization. Simi-larly, teachers understand better how their individual goals interrelate with the school's goals.

Experience tells us that when we recognize these relationships and feel ourselves a part of them, the likelihood increases that we will iden-tify with them. This identification leads to a shared vision of school life and a sense of loyalty to the school's mission.

Cognitive science tells us that an objective of brain-based learning is to develop a sense of deeper meaning. This meaning requires an emo-tional investment as well as multiple associations at multiple levels (Jensen, 1995, p. 197). The impact of such learning makes it more likely that life in the school will become personally meaningful.

CREATING BRAIN-BASED LEARNING PARTNERSHIPS

To be truly successful, learning organizations must promote ways to connect themselves to the broader environment. By doing so, members of the learning community understand how their actions affect a variety of constituencies. Additionally, it helps school stakeholders to connect to each other, their vision, their work, and their community. The creation of a learning organization challenges stakeholders in the school to use their collective intelligence, ability to learn, and creativity to transform existing systems.

Parents as Partners

Schools that develop a trusting, nurturing climate and seek and value parent involvement benefit everyone within the school community. Sub-stantial evidence exists to show that children whose parents are involved in their schooling demonstrate advanced academic achievement and cooperative development. Specifically, Lintos (1992) summarizes the positive outcomes for children as a result of parent involvement in their schooling to include: improved achievement, improved behavior, greater motivation, more regular attendance, lower dropout rates, and more positive attitudes toward homework.

Similarly, research indicates that parents also benefit from involvement in their child's education. Specifically, the parent-child relationship is improved, and parents become better teachers of their children (Henderson, 1988). Additionally, involved parents tend to develop positive attitudes about themselves, increase their own self-concepts (Becher, 1986), appreciate the efforts of teachers, and provide an overall higher rating of teachers' abilities (Lintos, 1992).

Given the significant contributions that parents can make toward their children's education and the success of the school, it is critical that they become active participants and learners. As active participants within the learning community, parents must also appreciate the benefits of brain-based learning. In general, parents must understand that the brain learns best in a sensory-rich immersion environment and that love, positive feedback, and opportunities for exploration and physical nurturing are also critical to their children's brain development.

Jensen (1995, pp. 343–344) has developed a parent checklist that helps parents provide their children with a brain-compatible learning environment.

1. Do you share something wondrous and exciting every day with your children that you personally learned during the day? If so, that enhances the positive value of learning.
2. Do you take your children to events that are designed specifically for learning? These things provide the critical opportunities to develop learning skills.
3. Do you speak of school and your job as a joyful adventure? Or do you more often refer to the headaches, the unmotivated learners, the late hours, the "TGIF" attitude, that is, the countdown until Friday, the next holiday, or summer?
4. Is your home a rich, positive learning environment, full of challenge, novelty, and ways to learn, such as with a computer, games, toys, cards, art, and music?
5. Do you avoid sarcasm, negative remarks, and criticism? Do you believe 100 percent in your children's potential? Do you daily affirm their gifts, their genius?

6. Do you provide affection, warmth, or other signs of your love for them? Are genuine compliments given? Or do your children get only an occasional pat on the back?

7. Is the television used sparingly, as much for learning as for entertainment? Or has it become just a babysitter, full of craziness, violence, and empty sitcoms packed with put-downs? What is really learned from it?

8. Do you take your children with you on trips, in the car, by bus or plane? Do you explore, discover, and get excited about life, animals, plants, and people?

9. Have you eliminated the use of threats in your family? Or do your kids do what they have to do because the alternatives are "or else!"?

10. Do you recount, revise, and review family activities? Do you encourage your children to do the same? This builds strong positive memories. Do you offer your kids a choice (whenever appropriate) of things to do and how to do them? Is there always hope? Do you talk positively about the future and its options?

11. Are your children getting adequate, stress-free rest, feeling safe and secure?

12. Is their daily food good for the brain? Do you ensure that your children have protein for breakfast, eat apples, eggs, bananas, wheat germ, lean meats, leafy green vegetables, and a diet low in polyunsaturated fats (no saturated ones)?

In utilizing such a list, parents begin to develop connections between the role of the school and the role of the home in providing a brain-friendly learning environment. This can be further enhanced by inviting parents to participate in relevant professional development activities at the school and/or increase their knowledge of brain-friendly techniques by sharing publications about how the brain develops and learns.

Intraorganization Partners

It is important to understand that learning partnerships extend beyond the walls of the schools. As resources for school improvement efforts shrink and the issues facing children and schools become more complex, it becomes increasingly important to extend the definition of community of learners to include organizations and institutions that can enrich school learning opportunities.

These organizations can include neighboring colleges and universities, local civic associations, senior citizen groups, and representatives from local government. The basis for their involvement is focused on the premise that all people benefit from being continual learners. Similarly, schools can better identify the expectations and needs of the constituencies they serve. In doing so, schools will better develop a measurement system that compares their vision with the vision of the community they serve.

The integration of this type of systems approach to enhance the community of learners creates a mutually beneficial partnership. Schools reap the benefits of collective planning and increase opportunities for financial and conceptual support. The institutions and organizations develop a sense of belonging within the school community and become a meaningful partner in the education of the community's children.

Students as Partners

Although the activities of all the adults within the learning community are ultimately centered on enriching learning experiences for students, rarely are students taught the skills to participate or are invited into the learning community. Above all else, students must be taught the importance of being lifelong learners. Additionally, teaching students about the way their brains learn and respond to different learning situations provides a foundation for students to think about how they think and act. Similarly, students can be taught that just as the brain constantly monitors the body, the brain benefits from a healthy body. Thus, the benefits of nutrition, exercise, and music to healthy brain development should play an important part in the student's understanding of learning.

Finally, students can be taught the importance of emotions in learning; that is, the limbic system, the primitive brain that neither reads nor writes, provides the feeling of what is real, true, and important (MacLean, 1990). The limbic system also controls impulsivity and aggression. Importantly, students can practice strategies for conflict resolution that are consistent with neurobiological research.

Sylwester (1996) concludes that in order to teach even the youngest children about how their brain learns, it is important to use a model they can understand. The triune brain model created by Dr. Paul MacLean is one such model to use. It divides the brain into three parts—the cerebral cortex, the limbic system and the brain stem—and relates how each part functions in the learning process. The limbic system is the gatekeeper for the brain and filters all entering information. Parts of the limbic system process the information, depending on whether or not the person "feels" safe. The information can go in three directions. It can remain in the limbic system, it can go into the cerebral cortex for slow processing and building of mental programs, or it can go into the brain stem, where our automatic "fight-or-flight" system assumes control. This model is over-simplified but is useful in helping students understand that the cerebral cortex must be involved when they are engaged in learning. They need to understand how their emotions can take control of their thinking, resulting in little or no cognitive processing and building of mental programs. Teachers can help students understand their emotions and the results of negative emotions on the ability of the cerebral cortex to use the information to build mental programs. Positive emotions, such as love, excitement, enthusiasm, and joy, enhance the ability of the cerebral cortex to process information and create permanent mental programs.

Teachers and Administrators as Partners

Probably the most important partnership within the school is the one that exists between the teacher and the principal. Throughout this book an emphasis has been placed on the significance of collaboration and team learning. These circumstances are necessary to develop a brain-friendly climate in which teachers instruct and principals administer in a manner that is consistent with what is known about the brain.

To that end, administrators must play a significant role in developing a school climate that fosters security, innovation, and a culture for continual learning. In turn, teachers create a rich environment where students have the ability to actively process learning in a nonthreatening setting.

Current research cites the benefits of principals who lead from the center rather than the top (Louis, Kruse, and Raywid, 1996) and the capacity of the staff to function as a professional learning community. Dufour (1999) describes behaviors that principals utilize to promote learning organizations. They include:

- Leading through shared vision and values rather than rules and procedures
- Enlisting faculty members in school decision-making processes and empowering individuals to act
- Providing the staff with the information, training, and parameters to make good decisions
- Being result-oriented
- Concentrating on posing the right questions rather than imposing solutions

Above all else, principals must create a culture of inquiry, where teachers (and other members of the learning community) are encouraged to develop their own capacity for leadership and continual learning. This can only happen when the principal nurtures a safe environment where: (1) group members get to know one another and build trusting relationships, (2) teachers are given the opportunity, time, and resources to reflect, research, and collaborate, and (3) teachers are encouraged to actively process what they have learned to solve relevant classroom and school problems.

SUMMARY

This chapter described and provided an operational blueprint for the establishment of schools as continual learning communities; places where people collectively create and take responsibility for their shared future; places where the emphasis is not on developing one's own territory or privileges, but where people collaborate to address system-wide problems and issues.

These organizations are characterized by:

- A strong sense of purpose that provides meaning for its existence
- A shared vision that provides a blueprint for action and change

- Individual empowerment to invest in and commit to the organization's purpose and vision
- A commitment to continual learning that provides the knowledge, skills, and resources to successfully pursue the organization's purpose and vision
- Appropriate support mechanisms where both individuals and organizational policies enable all group members to sustain the necessary effort to fulfill the organization's purpose and vision

Most importantly, learning organizations provide a way for individuals within the school to collaborate as a community to create a system that studies and implements strategies that make their school highly effective places for children to learn. Moreover, using what is known about brain-based learning should provide the foundation for how the members of the learning community plan for improvements in curriculum, instruction, assessment, and, importantly, the organizational climate of the school.

The cultivation of learning communities where all members value and model a passion for continual learning is critical to the success of our schools. As Marshall and Tucker (1992, p. xii) state, "The future now belongs to societies that organize themselves for learning."

REFERENCES

Becher, Rhoda. (1986). "Parents and Schools." *ERIC Digest,* Urbana, IL: ERIC Clearinghouse on Elementary and Early Childhood Education.

Brandt, Ron. (1998). *Powerful Learning.* Alexandria, VA: Association for Supervision and Curriculum Development.

Caine, Renate N. and Geoffrey Caine. (1991). *Making Connections: Teaching the Human Brain.* Alexandria, VA: Association for Supervision and Curriculum Development.

Dufour, Richard P. (1999). "Help Wanted: Principals Who Can lead Professional Learning." *NASSP,* 83 (604), 12–17.

Evans, Robert. (1996). *The Human Side of School Change.* San Francisco: Jossey-Bass.

Glickman, Carl. (1993). "Promoting Good Schools: The Core of Professional Work." General Assembly Presentation, Association of Supervision and Curriculum Development Annual Convention, Washington, DC.

————. (1992). *Supervision in Transition: 1992 Yearbook of the Association for Supervision and Curriculum Development.* Alexandria, VA: Association for Supervision and Curriculum Development.

Henderson, A. (October, 1988). "Parents Are a School's Best Friend." *Phi Delta Kappan,* 148–153.

Jensen, Eric. (1995). *Brain-Based Learning and Teaching.* Del Mar, CA: Turning Point Publishing.

Kaufman, Roger and Jerry Herman. (1991). *Strategic Planning in Education: Rethinking, Restructuring, and Revitalizing.* Lancaster, PA: Technomic Publishing Company.

Lashway, Larry. (1997). *Leading with Vision.* Eugene, OR: ERIC Clearinghouse on Educational Management, University of Oregon.

Lintos, Lynn Balster. (1992). *At-Risk Families and Schools Becoming Partners.* Eugene, OR: ERIC Clearinghouse on Educational Management.

Louis, Karen Seashore, Sharon Kruse, and Mary Anne Raywid. (1996). "Putting Teachers at Center of Reform." *NASSP Bulletin,* 83 (604), 12–17.

MacLean, Paul. (1990). *The Tribune Brain in Education.* New York: Plenum Press.

Marquardt, Michael J. (1996). *Building the Learning Organization.* New York: McGraw-Hill.

Marshall, R. and M. Tucker. (1992). *Thinking for Living: Education and the Wealth of Nations.* New York: Basic Books.

O'Keefe, J. and L. Nadel. (1978). *The Hypocampus as a Cognitive Map.* Oxford, England: Clarendon Press.

Scardamalia, M. and C. Berester. (1991). "Higher Levels of Agency for Children in Knowledge Building: A Challenge for the Design of New Knowledge Media." *Journal of the Learning Sciences,* 1, 37–68.

Senge, Peter M. (1990). *The Fifth Discipline: The Art and Practice of the Learning Organization.* New York: Doubleday.

Sylwester, Robert. (1996). *Celebrating Neurons: An Educator's Guide to the Human Brain.* Alexandria, VA: Association for Supervision and Curriculum Development.

Watkins, Karen E. and Victoria J. Marsick. (1999). "Sculpting the Learning Community: New Forms of Working and Organizing." *NASSP Bulletin,* 83 (604), 78–87.

Toward a Brain-Compatible Theory on School Reform

We can have superb schools if we go down new paths to get them. We can stay on solid ground throughout our quest. We have enough knowledge of the brain and experience in applying it to start now and quickly obtain gratifying results.

Leslie Hart

The 1990s was the Decade of the Brain. The twenty-first century is our opportunity to apply what we have learned. It will be a time to test our ability, as professionals, to act upon the wealth of information that has been generated and is continuing to be generated about the brain and human learning. Government agencies, medical researchers, universities, foundations, professional associations, and advocacy groups have raised the public's awareness of brain-related research and the implications of that research as it relates to education. It has been written about in national magazines and discussed on television news programs and talk shows and has been debated in the professional literature to the extent that it has increased "a simmering (professional) interest in the brain to the boiling point" (Bruer, May 1999). It can only be a matter of time until this interest in human cognition becomes the basis upon which educators will be expected to act and upon which the demands for school reform will be focused. Educators not only will be expected to know about the brain and how it learns but will soon be required to design curriculum, instruction, assessment, classrooms, and school organizations in ways that are demonstrably brain compatible.

What we now know and understand about human learning tends to support our instincts and our past experience with what works. It lends credibility to the so-called "progressive educational reforms" and supports the general consensus that the factory model of schools has failed. Teachers can no longer be the interpreters and disseminators of knowledge, and students can no longer be evaluated on how much they absorb and retain, unless we are willing to ignore the emerging body of science now available on how we learn. Brain-compatible teaching and learning favors a constructivist approach, an active learning model in which students are engaged in the learning process and in guiding their own instruction. We now know the importance of teaching for meaning and pattern detection, the route to understanding and retention, the importance of emotion and prior experience to future learning, the need for active and complex learning experiences, and the necessity of a non-threatening and highly challenging classroom environment. But can this knowledge from the biological and neurological sciences be organized into a coherent theory of teaching and learning that will serve as the catalyst for reform? Can this theory replace long-held misconceptions about learning and lead us to a new American school for the twenty-first century? The answer must be an emphatic *yes*.

No one would deny that teachers should be teaching and schools should be organized in ways that contribute to the students' understanding of and their ability to act upon the increasingly complex world in which they live. What we have assumed from psychology and the behavioral sciences, which have through observation given us insight into the functioning of the mind, can now be combined with the hard science of neurology, which has delineated how our brains develop and the process by which we learn. This synthesis of the science behind our behaviors and our tradition of basing our decisions about teaching on those behaviors provides us with a unique opportunity to create a new foundation upon which to base future school reform.

Brain research gives us the hard biological data, which allows us to make definitive recommendations about learning and the nature of the environment in which learning should take place. However, as Bruer (May 1999) cautions, it has a "seductive appeal" that tempts educators to be overly speculative about the application of the evidence available. As Joseph Le Doux warns us, "These ideas are easy to sell to the public, but

it is easy to take them beyond their actual basis in science" (p. 127). Educators, like all professionals, should be interested in knowing how brain research might contribute to the improvement of professional practice. But we must also be conscious, as Bruer (May, 1999) warns us, "that it is exceedingly difficult to separate the science from the speculation, to sort what we know from what we would like to be the case" (p. 650).

TOWARD A NEW FOUNDATION

Any progress toward a new theory of teaching and learning and school organization should be based on the biology of human learning. It must organize for us what is known and should provide direction for determining:

- What we should continue to do
- What we should no longer do
- What we should begin to do differently
- What areas should be further explored

The new theory should define to the best of our knowledge what learning is and explain how it comes about. And it must provide a structure for the design of curriculum frameworks, instructional strategies, assessment measures, and a style of classroom management that are compatible with what Leslie Hart calls the "natural functioning of the brain."

The demand on public education to prepare students for the twenty-first century is a dramatic departure from the mission for which the American system of public education was originally designed over one hundred years ago. More students than ever before will need to be equipped at a level of skill and knowledge that was formally reserved for only the best and the brightest. These changes in expectation come at a time when the fastest-growing segments of the student population (immigrant, poor, and minority students) are those with whom our schools have been historically least successful.

America's demographics and the rigors of preparing students for the new millennium will require a dramatic change in what we teach, how we are teaching it, and how we measure student performance. Those changes will need to be made on a school-wide basis, but at the classroom level. Teachers will need to be equipped with a comprehensive theory of teaching and learning that will enable them to rethink every aspect of the educational process, in terms not only of what they are doing but how they are getting things done. As Leslie Hart (1998) writes, "The system we attempt to keep using was never meant to deal with our present needs" (p. 308). It was also designed without the benefit of our present knowledge base about the brain. If schools are really going to prepare students for the 90,000 or more occupations that will be available to them schools will have to operate within the broadest terms, with a high degree of flexibility, and with the goal of continuing learning. Educators will need to work collectively as professionals and with the community using a unifying theory of human learning to make their decisions. They will need to be prepared to abandon those concepts, beliefs, traditions, and assumptions that obscure or conflict with what we are learning from current brain research. Schools that recognize and are compatible with the natural functioning of the brain will allow learning to take place more quickly, will deepen the students' understanding and retention of what has been learned, and will ultimately prove more successful in terms of the level of student performance.

Throughout this text we have emphasized much of the knowledge base upon which these educational decisions can and should be made to provide a learning environment that is viewed as compatible with the biology of human learning. It will require of both students and staff a working knowledge of the brain's physiology as it relates to how we learn, a rationale for challenging our current mental models of teaching and learning, and an exploration of how schools might better be organized and why. We have examined the issue of capturing and holding the brain's attention and the role that both emotion and prior experience play in determining meaning and ultimately storing and retaining what has been learned. We have discussed brain-compatible instruction and curriculum and the staff development required to support it. And we have detailed the school organization and climate of the learning organization required to sustain it. But how do these pieces come together as a blueprint for change, for building the knowledge base and organizational structure to create a brain-compatible school? How do we decide what is to be changed, what should be maintained and what new directions are worthy of pursuit?

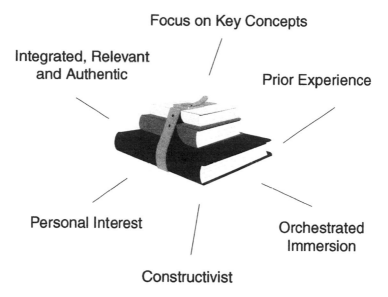

Focus on Key Concepts

Integrated, Relevant
and Authentic

Prior Experience

Personal Interest

Orchestrated
Immersion

Constructivist

Figure 9.2 The Nature of the Learning

The Nature of the Learner

What do we know about learning from brain research? We know that learning is the construction of meaning by the learner that results in a reorganization of the brain's connections among discrete pieces of information and previous networks. It is this reorganization that creates or adds to the complexity of existing programs the learner uses to understand and act upon future experiences. The process is a mind-body experience that is unique to the individual and dependent upon what the learner already knows or has experienced. It requires active participation by the learner and is enhanced by multisensory inputs and by social interaction in enriched and complex learning experiences.

Emotions are inseparable from learning and, in fact, drive the student's ability to pay attention and to devote energy to the learning task.

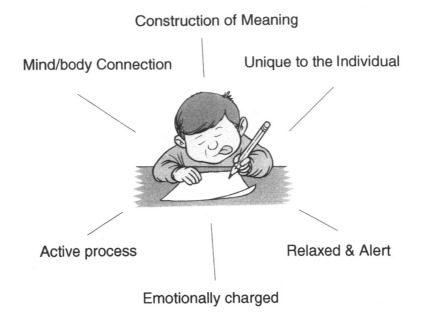

Construction of Meaning

Mind/body Connection

Unique to the Individual

Active process

Relaxed & Alert

Emotionally charged

Figure 9.1 *The Nature of the Learner*

A PORTRAIT OF BRAIN COMPATIBILITY

To understand the collective impact of what we now know about the brain and how it learns, it is important to consider both the nature of the learner and how that translates into the decisions we make about curriculum and assessment, instructional strategies, the climate of the classroom, and the organization of the school. The relationships among these elements, in terms of what we now know and what it means to current and future practice, are illustrated in figure 9.1. It is the combined effect of these elements that will create the brain-compatible environment we should be striving for. The attributes of each element can be used to assess the brain-compatible nature of what it is we are doing and what we should consider. Striving for small change, while an important first step, may require more energy and bring less progress than pursuing the larger aim of an eventual total reform.

Because our natural inclination is to only briefly attend to issues that are not critical to our survival, sustaining the students' attention may require a heavy reliance on personal meaning, relevance, knowledge of future use and novelty.

We know that learning cannot take place when the learner feels threatened and that the required cognitive processing of information is dramatically interfered with when students are either physically or psychologically stressed. In addition, students must be physically comfortable, have their physiological needs met (nutrition and rest), and be sufficiently challenged in order for learning to take place.

Learning is a messy process of pattern detection for which the brain is specifically designed. What we choose to attend to and what we select to remember is determined by both the quality of our initial experience and the opportunities we have to meaningfully process what it is we are trying to learn. Learning takes time and can be enhanced or inhibited by both the quality and the quantity of the feedback that the learner receives.

We learn best when we are relaxed and alert, and we learn the most from an immersion in relevant experiences that are challenging and authentic and personally meaningful.

The Nature of the Learning

Using what we know about the nature of the learner and how the brain learns provides some critical attributes around which brain-compatible curriculum can be built and/or evaluated. Our understanding of the brain and its natural tendencies toward learning supports a curriculum that is integrated, relevant, and authentic (see figure 9.2).

A brain-compatible curriculum must be based in the here and now, with an emphasis on the future use and transfer of what it is the students are expected to learn. The content of the curriculum should be expressed in terms of key concepts, and those concepts should be linked to the critical-thinking and reasoning skills that will provide the learner with the means to operationalize what it is they are expected to learn.

The curriculum should have specific outcomes or goals that are linked to the students' personal and/or prior experience and should be in a developmental sequence, whole to parts when applicable, so as to establish the relationships among concepts and curriculum areas.

Brain-compatible curriculums should be thematic and provide students with opportunities to make choices and take responsibility for the design and accomplishment of the learning activities in which they will be engaged. To be brain compatible, a curriculum or course of study should be based upon integrated, relevant, and authentic content. It must include complex experiences that provide the learners with the opportunities both to actively process what it is they are to learn and, from those experiences, to construct for themselves their personal meaning.

This constructivist approach to curriculum planning should utilize the available technology, be independent of traditional textbooks and publisher materials, and use all available primary sources and experiences. This will create an enriched and orchestrated immersion in which the students can experience to the extent practical the content and processes they are expected to learn.

A truly brain-compatible program of study should meet the individual needs of diverse students and evaluate their progress with a process of feedback and ongoing assessment that is authentic and an integral part of the curriculum and instruction being presented.

The Instruction

To say we are "teaching to the brain" is redundant, since the brain is the organ by which we learn, and the objective of teaching is to cause learning. Teaching in ways, however, that are compatible with how the brain learns is a significant departure from what many students experience and what many teachers currently plan for. What we now know about the human mind suggests that many of our instructional strategies are inconsistent with the brain's natural tendencies. The teacher-centered and teacher-directed classroom activities commonplace in most schools use strategies that ignore the students' needs for input, engagement, processing, feedback, and the construction of personal meaning that are critical to how they learn (see figure 9.3).

If, as we believe, learning is a mind/body experience in which our brain's natural tendency is to focus for short periods of time on those things that are of immediate importance or of personal interest to us, it is easy to see that much of what teachers do and expect their students to do is at least incompatible with and may even be antagonistic to how

Social Interaction

Active Participation

Student Choice
& Responsibility

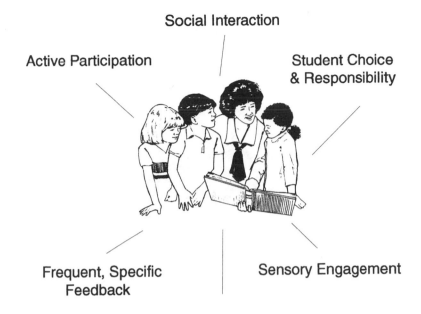

Frequent, Specific
Feedback

Sensory Engagement

Processing Time

Figure 9.3 *The Nature of Instruction*

students learn. Sitting and listening, symbol manipulation, acquiring content absent of context, following logical presentations, and rote memorization are among the activities and skills furthest removed from the students' natural tendencies.

In order to capitalize on the natural operation of the brain, instruction should be paced to the students' need for shifts in emphasis, opportunities for movement, active participation, and social interaction. Teaching strategies that use active sensory engagement and allow students to work collaboratively with the teacher as facilitator are far superior to more teacher-centered, didactic instructional styles, where the students are more passive and the role of the teacher is more directive.

Processing time is critically important to the learning process and is not always provided by the completion of worksheets or seat work

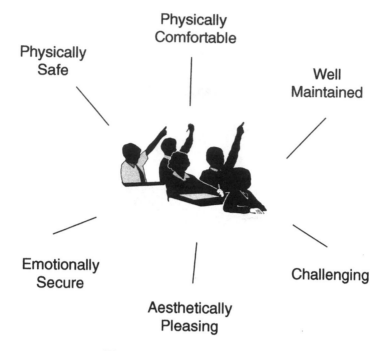

Figure 9.4 *The Nature of the Climate*

assignments that are designed to structure the students' responses. Far more conducive to the learning process are work groups that involve the student with other students, the teacher, and even other adults in the classroom in a variety of activities that include production of group projects, writing exercises, use of role plays, simulations, and field experiences.

When students are called upon to construct their personal meaning from less active classroom experiences, special attention should be paid to structuring those experiences, to the extent possible, to the brain's need for input and pattern-seeking tendencies. Techniques such as advanced organizers, overviews, identification of main ideas, and connection to personal experience and prior learning should be incorporated.

Equally important to the nature of the instruction is the frequency and nature of the feedback that students receive on their progress. Student feedback should be frequent, immediate, and specific in order to hold the students' attention and to assist them in mastering the knowledge and skills they are attempting to acquire. Students can benefit from having the opportunity to choose from a variety of assignments and will learn more naturally from the elaborate rehearsal of the learning than from more traditional, repetitive practice exercises.

Brain-compatible instruction, like the brain-compatible curriculum it is designed to deliver, builds upon the students' natural tendencies and addresses the need for unique classroom experiences intended to meet the very individual learning needs of each student.

The Climate

Perhaps the greatest difference between the school as we know it and the brain-compatible classroom and school is the increased attention that needs to be paid to the classroom climate. Classrooms need to be physically safe and comfortable and must provide a nonthreatening yet challenging educational climate (see figure 9.4).

The classroom itself should be an inviting environment, both physically and psychologically. Students and the teacher need to feel safe in order to focus on the educational process. As we have seen, threats, either physical or psychological, cause the brain to "downshift" and interfere with and inhibit its capacity to learn.

Equally important to the efficient functioning of the brain is the physical environment and the satisfaction of the learners' physiological needs. Classrooms must be clean, comfortable, well maintained, and aesthetically pleasing. Students need to be well rested, well fed, and healthy. Attention should be paid in designing classrooms and instructional activities to the students' needs for movement, short rest breaks, and lavatory breaks and to recognizing the importance of drinks and snacks to their mental alertness.

The role of emotion in the learning process also takes on a greater significance when we apply brain research to learning and the climate of the classroom. The classroom must be both a nonthreatening environment in which students are encouraged to take risks and a venue in which significant relationships with the teacher and fellow students are encouraged. Teachers can do this through management of their own interactions with individual students and the types of interactions they encourage among the students in the class. The brain-compatible classroom is characterized by the reduction of anxiety, which can be brought about through the effective use of praise, the elimination of threats, opportunities for celebration, and the acknowledgement of success. This classroom also provides students with choices and experiences that allow them to take responsibility for their own challenges and assessment. Such classrooms are characterized by low threat, high challenge, rich and varied inputs, and relaxed alertness.

The Organization

The ultimate goal for using what we are learning about learning through brain research is to build a school organization that is compatible with brain functioning, for both the students and the teachers. While differences exist between students and adult learners, the basic tenets of our brain functioning vary very little over the course of our lives. This means, of course, that the same principles of attention and retention, the role of emotion, and the nature of the learning environment required for optimal learning by the students are required for adults if we expect their continued professional growth.

Professional staff at all levels need to understand the underlying biological and neurological science that can now serve as the basis for an effective theory of human learning and must use that information as they make decisions about the mission, organization, operation, and assessment of the school. School organizations need to present a coherence of purpose that reflects our most current understanding of human behavior and brain functioning. They must have a shared vision of what the school is and what it can become. A priority must be placed on community involvement and staff collaboration so that the nature of the learning environment that we are striving for within the classroom can be modeled for the students through the behavior of the adults in the learning organization (see figure 9.5).

The outcome of these efforts is to create continuous learning envi-

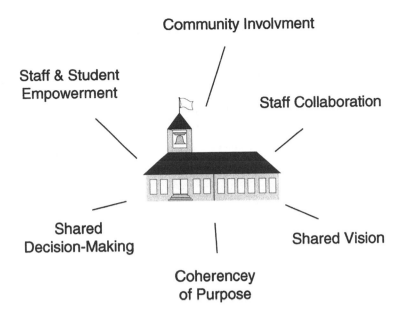

Figure 9.5 *The Nature of the Organization*

ronments where individuals transform themselves as the organization transforms itself. In creating such an environment, the major stakeholders within the school community work collaboratively to search for meaning, inquire systematically, and learn collectively.

The characteristics of such an environment will be focused on several interrelated elements. While each element, in and of itself, has benefits, recognition must be given to the interconnectedness of the elements as they are implemented within the parameters of school life. Central to these elements is an acknowledgment of the importance of a physical and emotional environment that empowers members of the school community to seek opportunities to contribute to the learning environment. Secondly, through the established opportunities for collaboration and team learning, a shared vision is crafted that provides focus and energy for ongoing shared learning.

Finally, it is critical that the members of the learning community recognize and value the patterns that connect what they are doing to the larger system. Through the development of a perceptual map of the relationships between what individuals do and the overall mission of the school, all stakeholders become aware of how they fit within the "big picture." In doing so, stakeholders better understand how their individual work adds to the collective work of the organization. Similarly, they better understand how their individual goals interrelate with the school's goals.

NEXT STEPS

Creating a brain-compatible learning organization is not something that can be done overnight or in a particular way for every school. Like the individuals who comprise a school, each organization has its own methods and pace of progress toward becoming a learning organization, a school that will enhance rather than inhibit the process of education. But despite the absence of a single blueprint for improvement, we should not hesitate to apply what we know and are constantly learning to the improvement of our current educational practice. Educators and the other stakeholders must strive to bring about improvement by applying what we know works and by abandoning those practices we now know no longer work, such as lecturing, telling and demonstrating, seatwork, recitation, and rote learning. We need to pursue those areas of educational research that show promise. In our quest to bring about improvement we must make our decisions about what to teach, how to teach and assess what is learned, and how to organize our classrooms and schools based what we now know about brain compatibility. The relationship among the key elements we have discussed is illustrated in figure 9.6.

These elements can be used as criteria for evaluating the growing number of materials advertised as "brain compatible." They can help educators reach decisions related to curriculum, instruction, assessment, scheduling, and professional development, as well as the many other factors that are a part of developing a school organization that will accelerate student learning. In total, they represent a learning culture that keeps both students and teachers relaxed and alert, challenged but not

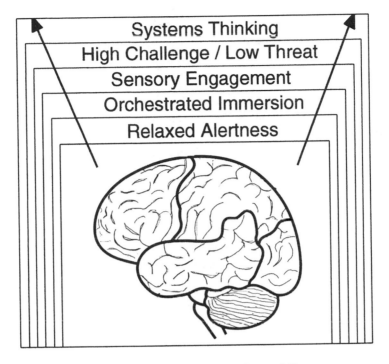

Figure 9.6 *A Portrait of Brain Compatibility*

threatened, and immersed in activities that are designed to assist them in the natural process of constructing meaning from their experiences.

The information provided in this text and the bibliography that follows represents a comprehensive compilation of the available information that should serve as the basis for your own exploration of the science of the brain and how it can be applied to your classroom or school.

While no single design for a brain-compatible school should be followed, certain common characteristics are likely to be among the attributes of those attempts that are most successful. Brain compatibility will more likely be found in classrooms:

- That are organized with flexible, temporary groupings
- In which teachers work as teams

- Where instructional patterns are student directed
- Where lockstep activities for the whole class are replaced with individual and group pursuits of knowledge guided
- Where teachers guide learning based on perceived student needs and interests

The curriculum will no longer be represented by an accumulation of courses and credits measured in grade levels and seat time but by demonstrated competence in broad areas of skills and behaviors. Content will be organized by themes rather than disciplines, and performance and experience will be given emphasis over the acquisition of factual knowledge and discrete information.

Students will work collaboratively with each other and with a variety of adults as they are actively engaged in sensory experiences rather than passive recipients of information disseminated by the teacher, and student progress will be individualized and outcome based. The school community itself will become what Leslie Hart calls "a learning center for all" (Hart, 1998, p. 354).

To make this transition will be no easy task. The professional staff, the students themselves, and the community that the school serves cannot be expected to change overnight their long-held beliefs and expectations about learning. They will need time to absorb the new perspective presented by brain research, to reflect on it, and to plan collectively for the changes it implies. They will need both permission to abandon their traditional practices and behaviors and encouragement to take risks. And as with all learning, they will need feedback on their efforts that is specific and immediate enough to result in continued improvement. Last and perhaps most important, practitioners will need protection from the inevitable criticism that comes with change and a strong defense of the effort to bring about a more brain-compatible learning environment.

What we now know about teaching and learning, while still not a complete theory, can be used to guide us in designing instruction, curriculum, and school organizations that are much more likely to improve student performance. It is a path that every educator must be encouraged to pursue.

Students and Our Classrooms." *NASSP Bulletin,* Reston, VA: National Association of Secondary School Principals. 82 (598), 29–37.

Lashway, Larry. (1997). *Leading with Vision.* Eugene, OR: ERIC Clearinghouse on Educational Management, University of Oregon.

Le Doux, Joseph. (1996). *The Emotional Brain: The Mysterious Underpinnings Of Emotional Life.* New York: Simon and Schuster.

Leithwood, Kenneth. (1992). "The Move Toward Transformational Leadership." *Educational Leadership,* 49 (5), 34–35.

Lieberman, A. (1995). "Practices That Support Teacher Development." *Phi Delta Kappan,* 76 (8), 591–596.

Lintos, Lynn Balster. (1992). *At-Risk Families and Schools Becoming Partners.* Eugene, OR: ERIC Clearinghouse on Educational Management.

Little, Judith W. (1981). "The Power of Organizational Setting: School Norms and Staff Development." Paper presented at the annual meeting of the American Educational Research Association, Los Angeles, CA.

———. (1982). "Norms of Collegiality and Experimentation: Workplace Conditions of School Success." *American Educational Research Journal,* 19 (3), 325–340.

Lortre, D. C. (1975). *Schoolteacher: A Sociological Study.* Chicago, IL: University of Chicago Press.

Louis, Karen Seashore, Sharon Kruse, and Mary Anne Raywid. (1996). "Putting Teachers at Center of Reform." *NASSP Bulletin,* 83 (604), 12–17.

MacLean, Paul. (1990). *The Tribune Brain in Education.* New York: Plenum Press.

Margulies, Nancy. (1991). *Mapping Inner Space: Learning and Teaching Mindmapping.* Tucson, AZ: Zephyr Press.

Marquardt, Michael J. (1996). *Building the Learning Organization.* New York: McGraw-Hill.

Marshall, R. and M. Tucker. (1992). *Thinking for Living: Education and the Wealth of Nations.* New York: Basic Books.

Marshall, Stephanie Pace. (May, 1998). "Creating Pioneers for an Unknown Land: Education for the Future." *NASSP Bulletin,* Reston, VA: National Association of Secondary School Principals. 82 (598), 48–55.

Maute, J. (1992). "Cross-Curricular Connections." In *Connecting the Curriculum Through Interdisciplinary Instruction,* edited by J. H. Lounsbury. Columbus, OH: National Middle School Association.

Miere, Deborah. (Summer, 1992). "Reinventing Teaching." *Teachers College Record.* New York: Teachers College Press.

Ogden, Evelyn H. and Vito Germinario. (1995). *The Nation's Best Schools:*

Blueprints for Excellence. Volume 2, *Middle and Secondary School.* Lancaster, PA: Technomic Publishing Company.

O'Keefe, J. and L. Nadel. (1978). *The Hypocampus as a Cognitive Map.* Oxford, England: Clarendon Press.

Perkins, Peggy G. and Jeffrey I. Gelfer. (1993). "Portfolio Assessment for Teachers." *The Clearing House,* 66 (4), 235–237.

Peters, Thomas. (1987). *Thriving on Chaos.* New York: Alfred A. Knopf.

Pilon, G. H. (1991). *Workshop Way.* New Orleans: Workshop Way Incorporated.

Pounder, Diana G. and Rodney T. Ogawa. (1995). "Leadership as an Organization-wide Phenomenon: Its Impact on School Performance." *Educational Administrative Quarterly,* 31 (4), 564–588.

Richardson, Michael D., Kenneth E. Lane, and L. Jackson. (1995). *School Empowerment.* Eugene, OR: Technomic Publishing Company.

Roberts, N. (1985). "Transforming Leaders: A Process of Collective Action." *Human Relations,* 38 (11), 1023–1046.

Rosenfield, I. (1988). *The Invention of Memory.* New York: Basic Books.

Ross, Ann and Karen Olsen. (1993). *The Way We Were . . . The Way We Can Be: A Vision for the Middle School Through Integrated Thematic Instruction,* 2d ed. Kent, WA: Books for Educators, Covington Square.

Sagar, Richard D. (1992). *How to Conduct Collaborative Action Research.* Alexandria, VA: Association for Supervision and Curriculum Development.

———. (1992). "Three Principals Who Make a Difference." *Educational Leadership,* 49 (5), 13–18.

Scardamalia, M. and C. Berester. (1991). "Higher Levels of Agency for Children in Knowledge Building: A Challenge for the Design of New Knowledge Media." *Journal of the Learning Sciences,* 1, 37–68.

Senge, Peter M. (1990). *The Fifth Discipline: The Art and Practice of the Learning Organization.* New York: Doubleday.

Shoemaker, Betty Jean Eklund. (October, 1989). "Integrative Education. A Curriculum for the Twenty-First Century." *OSSC Bulletin,* 33 (2).

Shubert, William H. (1993). "Curriculum Reform." *Challenges and Achievements of American Education,* Alexandria, VA: The Association for Supervision and Curriculum Development. 80–84.

Shuell, T. "Cognitive Conceptions of Learning." *Review of Educational Research,* 56, 411–436.

Sylwester, Robert. (Unpublished). "Intelligence—What It Is, How to Enhance It."

———. (Unpublished). "Memory—Acquiring/Editing/Recalling/Forgetting."

———. (1995). *A Celebration of Neurons: An Educator's Guide to the Human*

Brain. Alexandria, VA: Association for Supervision and Curriculum Development.

———. (Summer, 1997). "Bioelectronic Learning: The Effects of Electronic Media on the Developing Brain." *Tecnos,* 6 (2), 19–22.

———. (January, 1998). "The Brain Revolution." *The School Administrator,* Arlington, VA: American Association of School Administrators. 55(1):6–10.

Smith, M. and J. O'Day. (1990). Position Paper on Education Reform Debate. Stanford, CA: Stanford University Center for Policy Resources in Education.

Smith, Stuart C. and James J. Scott. (1990). *A Work Environment for Effective Instruction.* Alexandria, VA: National Association of Secondary School Principals.

Sousa, David. (1998). *Learning Manual for How the Brain Works.* Thousand Oaks, CA: Corwin Press.

———. (December, 1998) "Is the Fuss about Brain Research Justified?" *Education Week.* 35, 52.

———. (January, 1998). "The Ramifications of Brain Research." *The School Administrator,* Alexandria, VA: American Association of School Administrators. 55 (1), 22–25.

Sparks, Dennis and Stephanie Hirsh. (1997). *A New Vision for Staff Development.* Alexandria, VA: Association for Supervision and Curriculum Development.

Speck, Marsha. (1996). "Best Practices in Professional Development." *ERS Spectrum,* 14 (2), 33–41.

Teaching and the Human Brain. Alexandria, VA: Association for Supervision and Curriculum Development.

Tonnensen, Sandra and Susan Patterson. (1992). "Fighting the First-Year Jitters." *The Executive Educator,* 14 (1), 29–30.

Uchida, Donna, Marion Cetron, and Floretta McKenzie. (1996). *Preparing Students for the Twenty-First Century.* Reston, VA: American Association of School Administrators.

"Understanding the Brain—Educators Seek to Apply Brain Research." (September, 1995). *Education Update Newsletter,* Alexandria, VA: Association for the Development of Supervision and Curriculum. 37 (7), 1, 4–5.

Valencia, S. W. and J. P. Killian. (1988). "Overcoming Obstacles to Teacher Change: Direction from School-Based Efforts." *Journal of Staff Development,* 9 (2), 168–174.

Valencia, Sheila, William McGinley, and P. David Pearson. (1990). "Assessing Reading and Writing: Building a More Complete Picture." In *Reading in the Middle School,* 2d ed., edited by Gerald Duffy. Newark, DE: International Reading Association.

Walker, Bradford L. (March, 1993). "What It Takes to Be an Empowering Principal." *Principal,* 41–42.

Watkins, Karen E. and Victoria J. Marsick. (1990). *In Action: Creating the Learning Organization,* Volume I. Alexandria, VA: American Society for Training and Development.

————. (1993). *Sculpting the Learning Organization: Lesson in the Art of Systemic Change.* San Francisco: Jossey-Bass.

————. (1999). "Sculpting the Learning Community: New Forms of Working and Organizing." *NASSP Bulletin,* 83 (604), 78–87.

Weber, Ellen. (May, 1998). "Marks of a Brain Based Assessment: A Practical Checklist." *NASSP Bulletin,* Reston, VA: National Association of Secondary School Principals. 82 (598), 63–72.

Wells, Scott. (November, 1992). "Interdisciplinary Learning—Movement to Link Discipline Gains Momentum." Alexandria, VA: ASCD Curriculum Update.

Wheatley, M. J. (1993). *Leadership and the New Science.* San Francisco: Berrett-Koehler.

Wolf, Pat. (1997) "Translating Brain Research into Educational Practice." Satellite Broadcast. Alexandria, VA: Association for Supervision and Curriculum Development.

Wurman, Richard Saul. (1989). *Information Anxiety.* New York: Doubleday.

Resources For Further Study

Armstrong, T. (1990). *Multiple Intelligences in the Classroom*. Alexandria, VA: ASCD.

Brandt, R. (1998). *Powerful Learning*. Alexandria, VA: Association for Supervision and Curriculum Development.

Brooks, Jacqueline Grennon and Martin G. Brooks. (1995). *The Case for Constructivist Classrooms*. Alexandria, VA: Association for Supervision and Curriculum Development.

Caine, R. and G. Caine. (1991). *Making Connections: Teaching and the Human Brain*. Alexandria, VA: Association for Supervision and Curriculum Development.

Caine, R. and G. Caine. (1997). *Education on the Edge of Possibility*. Alexandria, VA: Association for Supervision and Curriculum Development.

Calvin, William. (1996). *How Brains Think: Evolving Intelligence, Then and Now*. New York, NY: Basic Books.

Elias, M., Zins, E., Weissberg, R., Frey, K., Greenberg, M., Haynes, N., Kessler, R., and D. Goleman. (1995). *Emotional Intelligence*. New York, NY: Bantam Books.

Diamond, M. (1998). *Magic Trees of the Mind*. New York, NY: Dutton.

Gardner, Howard. (1991). *The Unschooled Mind: How Children Learn and How Schools Should Teach*. New York, NY: Basic Books.

Hannaford, Carla. (1995). *Smart Moves: Why Learning is Not All in Your Head*. Arlington, VA: Great Ocean Publishers.

Jensen, E. (1995). *The Learning Brain*. Del Mar, CA: Turning Point Publishing.

Jensen, E. (1996). *Brain Based Learning*. Del Mar, CA: Turning Point Publishing.

LeDoux, J. (1996). *The Emotional Brain*. New York, NY: Touchstone.

Pert, C. (1997). *Molecules of Emotion*. New York, NY: Scribner.

Pinker, Steven. (1997). *How the Mind Works*. NY: Norton Press.

Sousa, D. (1995). *How the Brain Learns*. Reston, VA: National Association of Secondary School Principals.

Sylwester, R. A *Celebration of Neurons: An Educators Guide to the Human Brain*. Alexandria, VA: ASSCD.

Torp, L. and S. Sage. (1998). *Problems and Possibilities*. Alexandria, VA: Association for Supervision and Curriculum Development.

Index

About the Authors

Dr. Henry Cram received his Ed.D from Rutgers University in Educational Administration and Supervision. He is currently Superintendent of the Rancocas Valley Regional School District in Mount Holly, New Jersey, and a part-time lecturer at the Graduate School of Education at Rutgers University. Dr. Cram has held several teaching and administrative positions at all levels of education and works as a consultant for the Middle States Association. He has presented workshops and provided consultant services to area school districts and professional associations and has authored several articles for state and national publications. His first book, *Change for Public Education: Practical Ideas for the 21st Century,* was published in 1998 and was coauthored with Dr. Germinario.

Dr. Vito Germinario received his Ed.D. from Rutgers University in Educational Administration and Supervision. He currently serves as Superintendent of Schools for the Moorestown Public Schools, Moorestown, New Jersey. He has teaching experience at the junior high, high school, and college levels. Dr. Germinario has been an elementary and middle school principal and an assistant superintendent. He lectures and conducts workshops for numerous schools throughout the United States and for professional organizations such as the Association for Supervision and Curriculum Development, the National Association for School Executives, and the National Association of Student Assistance Professionals. He has coauthored five books, including his most recent, *Change for Public Education: Practical Ideas for the 21st Century.*